Reassuring Guidance

A FAITH-BASED CAREGIVING RESOURCE

Roy Cook
with Catherine Hilliard

CrossLink Publishing
RAPID CITY, SD

Cook/CrossLink Publishing
1601 Mt Rushmore Rd. Ste 3288
Rapid City, SD 57701
www.CrossLinkPublishing.com

Ordering Information:
Quantity sales. Special discounts are available on quantity purchases by corporations, associations, and others. For details, contact the "Special Sales Department" at the address above.

Reassuring Guidance/Roy Cook. —1st ed.
ISBN 978-1-63357-240-9
Library of Congress Control Number: 2021945977

To the memory of Gwen, who was the inspiration for this book. She was a bright shining example to everyone she met of how placing your trust in God gives you the strength to face life's most turbulent storms knowing that a better future lies ahead.

—Roy

To my husband, Ron. Your gentle nudges, constant encouragement, and confidence in who I am have been so instrumental in my journey as a caregiver. Thank you for your prayers and support enabling me to put in writing what I have learned. Thank you for your reminders that God is with me in everything I do.

—Catherine

Lighthouses provide sure and steady service day after day and night after night. As a caregiver, with the help of others, you can provide the same consistent service. You can be a bright shining beacon, a welcome sight in a gathering storm, providing reassuring guidance, help, and comfort.

Contents

Preface

Has God entrusted a special person in need of care to you? Is the enormity of this task humbling? Are there days when you question your caregiving abilities? Do you want to be the best caregiver possible? Do you want to learn from other caregivers? If you answered yes to any of these questions, you're not alone. This book is for you.

I've listened to many caregivers who've found themselves dealing with these same questions and many more. While I searched for answers, a chance encounter with Catherine Hilliard led to a series of aha moments and insights. My wife, Gwen, and I first met Catherine at church. Over the years we simply exchanged pleasantries, knowing her as the pastor's wife. However, it wasn't until we attended one of her classes on developing spiritual practices that we started becoming better acquainted.

As I pushed Gwen's wheelchair through the door to her classroom, I was greeted by the sight of a room filled with at least twenty women deep in conversation. Catherine beamed a welcoming smile and invited us in, making room for Gwen's wheelchair in the over-filled room. I kept looking around the room for another man, but there wasn't one in sight.

I was definitely feeling out of place. However, since Gwen really wanted to attend this class, I decided to give it a try. We would be learning how to grow in our faith by developing spiritual practices as we read through the 23rd Psalm. One of the first questions Catherine asked as we started the class was, "Does anyone know anything about sheep?" Not being the bashful type, I raised my hand. There I was, the only man in a class full of women, and the only one to raise a hand. All of a sudden, I wished I hadn't raised my hand—or could at least slowly slip out of sight under the table. Rather than making me feel out of place, Catherine asked a few questions about my sheep-related experiences and then continued on with the lesson.

It quickly became evident that I was the only one in the class who had any practical knowledge about sheep, so she continued calling on me with a question about sheep every time we met. Testing my knowledge about sheep always put me on the spot, invariably bringing a smile to Gwen's face. It was easy to see from these interactions that a bond was forming among the three of us. Who would have known that an off-handed question about sheep could lead to a life-changing friendship focused on caregiving?

As Gwen's Parkinson's disease progressed, Catherine frequently stopped by our house. Her visits always served as a source of encouragement. The moment she stepped through the door, Gwen and I could immediately sense that she truly cared. She always arrived with a heartwarming smile and something fun in her hands. It felt a little bit like Christmas morning every time she arrived: there was always a surprise. We never knew what to expect. It could have been anything from a fresh baked loaf of sourdough bread or a special jam to a small bouquet of flowers or a crossword puzzle book. Her visits were always a comfort and an inspiration. She seemed to know instinctively when to come, what to say, how long to stay, how to pray for us, and how and when to make helpful suggestions that added joy to our lives.

As Gwen, Catherine, and I became better acquainted, our aha moments and insights about caregiving started coming together.

Catherine shared how the experiences of being a caregiver for her mother had inspired her to reach out to others in need of care. This desire helped her to step in and support other caregivers and their loved ones. We then began comparing notes on our experiences and noticed many similarities. It was through these conversations that we also came to realize the importance of faith in the lives of caregivers and their loved ones.

The heartfelt requests we heard from caregivers searching for guidance led us to the idea of writing a book. They were seeking a book that combined helpful caregiving insights with a faith-based approach. Based on our experiences and what we had learned from the personal, and often emotional, experiences of other long-term caregivers and their loved ones, *Reassuring Guidance: A Faith-Based Caregiving Resource* soon became a reality. In each chapter of this book, you'll find engaging and tender stories, practical advice, encouragement, and inspirational thoughts for immediate use and future reference.

We're writing from our experiences as caregivers. We aren't medical professionals, psychologists, or social workers. If you have medical questions or need professional assistance, seek qualified help. Don't be timid about reaching out to these professionals as you'll undoubtedly need help from many of them in your caregiving journey.

No matter where you are in your faith journey, we pray that you'll continue to grow in your walk with God and rest in the assurance that you can rely on Him. If you are concerned about taking on the responsibilities of caregiving, know that you can learn to help your loved one if you are willing to try. You don't have to face caregiving challenges on your own. You have the opportunity to learn and grow as you partner with God in caring for your loved one. Slip your hand into His as you go through each day. He will be there to give you the courage and strength to be the caregiver you want to be.

Acknowledgements

We would like to extend a heart-felt thank you to everyone who made this book possible. Without their encouragement, prayers, critical reviews, and thoughtful comments, we would never have successfully completed this project.

Melanie Chitwood
Chad and Sabrina Cook
Larry and Trish Corman
Jackson Eubank IV
Lisa Hawkins
Kenneth Hilgendorf Jr.
Ron Hilliard
Priscilla McKinnon
Reed and Joanne McKnight
Elizabeth Nielsen
Elliot Ott
Sara Parente
Terry Shimkus
Paul Wainwright
Peter and Lora Woods

CHAPTER ONE

The Journey

One who has journeyed in a strange land cannot
return unchanged.
C. S. Lewis

When did you notice that God had entrusted an increasingly dependent friend or loved one into your care? When did you join the tens of millions of people who face the daily challenges of caregiving? When did you add the role of caregiver to the one you already have as a spouse, friend, child, or companion? What does this new role entail?

No matter when this role began or what lies ahead, step forward with confidence knowing you have an opportunity to make a meaningful difference for someone depending on you. Take time along every step of this ever-changing journey to experience God's comforting presence. As He walks along beside you, He promises to be there providing the hope and strength to support and guide you through each day.

Whether these newfound responsibilities crept up on you or happened in the blink of an eye, there always seems to be so much to do and so many new things to learn. Begin by learning all you can about your loved one's prognosis and how their short-term and long-term caregiving requirements will change over time. This will be a time of discovery, some of it planned and some of it happening through sheer serendipity.

For me and my wife, Gwen, the need for caregiving crept up on us. There were some ever-so-subtle signs that changes were on the horizon and that caregiving was in my future. I could see the storm clouds gathering in my mind and even hear the low rumble of distant thunder in my heart. This was how I felt as we were sitting in the waiting area at the Mayo Clinic and anticipating what we might hear on our first visit with the neurologist. When she confirmed Gwen's Parkinson's disease diagnosis, there was no question that changes were coming. After she described the general prognosis of what we could expect, we were numb. Then, as the uncertainties and reality of this diagnosis began setting in, there were teary eyes, and all we could do was hug each other.

There was so much to talk about. What was Gwen feeling? What could I do to understand and relate to her fears and anxieties? How would I adjust to this new set of responsibilities? As we discussed our future, we agreed that there would be some major adjustments ahead, but we thought we'd have plenty of time to prepare.

Then, before I knew it, it seemed like the responsibilities of caregiving were piling up. They crept up on me just like one of those pop-up afternoon thunderstorms. Not knowing what to expect, we found ourselves wanting to be prepared while at the same time searching for our imaginary protective umbrellas of certainty to fend off the coming rainstorms of change.

Catherine experienced many of the same feelings as she found herself stepping in to care for her mother. There weren't watershed moments of needing to provide care for her in the beginning, just occasional requests for help here and there. However, over time these requests became more frequent. Before she knew it, she became the primary caregiver for her mother.

For our friend, Kenny, it was a different story. The need for caregiving just seemed to appear all of a sudden! He vividly remembers the first time he heard about his sister's frightening cancer diagnosis. He said, "When it happened to me, it was like being hit by a truck!" They were very close. He immediately knew he needed to carve out large blocks of time in his busy schedule to do everything possible to support her, her husband, and their children.

Kenny's comments brought back memories of when I unexpectedly learned that my once vibrant and active mother had stage-four cancer resulting from an improperly treated melanoma. When the doctor said, "Your mother has only a few months to live," the flood of emotions that hit me could only be dealt with in an uncontrollable torrent of blubbering sobs. There was no time to casually plan for inevitable changes.

Can you relate to any of these stories? Think about your current situation and see if any of the following sentiments sound familiar:

- Things like this only happen to other people, not us.
- Surely this will pass.
- If only the test results had been different.
- This can't be happening; we had plans.
- Shouldn't we get a second opinion?
- We can fight this. Maybe the doctors are wrong!
- If we pray harder, everything will be okay.

If there are other thoughts that come to mind, take time to add them to the list. No matter how and when these thoughts led to the realization that caregiving was needed, the emotional turmoil surrounding these feelings can be overwhelming.

Many unanswered questions as well as a stream of emotions ranging from anger, despair, and doubt to fear, sadness, and disbelief can easily engulf you when coming to grips with the idea of becoming a caregiver. New and often troubling thoughts about an uncertain future, fears, concerns, and feelings of helplessness can enter your mind and continue to linger. If you're becoming the keystone (primary 24/7) caregiver, those storm clouds of change will no longer just smell like rain: they'll begin turning into rainstorms of new responsibilities.

Trying to ignore these new feelings and demands won't make them go away. Just like an unannounced visitor, the need for caregiving seems to show up unexpectedly. When it does, you have a choice. You can either willingly accept this caregiving opportunity or begrudgingly tolerate its arrival. One approach is positive; the other is negative. We hope you'll choose the positive approach, seeing caregiving as an opportunity and not a burden.

By taking the first steps of this journey willingly and because you truly care, you can find meaningful fulfillment and joy as you learn, grow, and become more confident in your abilities. If you're reluctant, the opposite can also be true. If you enter your new role thinking of it as a burden, it can be physically and emotionally draining, leading to periods of unneeded drama. It can turn into a negative, self-fulfilling prophesy, slowly devolving into an inconvenience only to be endured.

Drawing on your faith and deciding to proactively face these challenges as an intentional caregiver allows you to find blessings in even the most difficult situations. One of these blessings is realizing that God is with you and your loved one every day. He will be your companion on this journey and promises to never leave you. He made each of us, knitting us together before we were born. He knows what's going on and happening in all our lives (Psalm 139). No matter what happens, trust God and His plans for you and the person you find yourself caring for. With God at your side, you don't have to face caregiving challenges on your own.

New Realities

Taking on caregiving responsibilities can bring back memories of caring for a baby. There you were, facing the responsibilities of caring for an infant who was completely dependent on you for everything. There was so much to learn. You searched for everything you could find on caring for babies. You also probably relied on family and friends for their assistance and helpful suggestions. More than likely, they offered words of assurance, telling you that you were doing a good job even when they might have known an easier way. They also answered a lot of what may now seem like silly questions.

The challenges were new, and you were eager to learn. You may not have done everything perfectly, but luckily your child never knew what you lacked in experience or knowledge. When you faced a new challenge, you learned on the job and adapted. When all else failed, you simply did your best and made up for what you didn't know with love, improvisation, and enthusiasm. The same types of experiences and a similar sense of fulfillment can be found in caregiving.

Neither the challenges of caring for a newborn nor of caring for someone who becomes dependent on you come with easy-to-follow directions. You can, however, get a realistic preview of what to expect by doing some research. You can talk to other caregivers, read about how to be a caregiver, look at YouTube videos, or search the internet for insights and advice dealing with commonly encountered challenges. This research can serve as a good starting point, providing basic caregiving information for things like monitoring medications, coordinating household chores, scheduling appointments, and fixing simple meals.

However, to be an intentional caregiver requires doing more than just providing for basic needs. You may need to learn new skills and grow into this new role. Observing and putting into practice what you learn from others in similar circumstances can take you to a higher level of caregiving. While observing these caregivers, ask questions and listen closely to their advice and suggestions. All the while actively seek out and lean on those who are willing to step in and walk along beside you. They can provide the much-needed comfort and support you and your loved one will need.

While Catherine and I were both blessed by growing up around some great caregiving role models, we also discovered new ones during our journeys. Through their prayers, words of affirmation, patient listening, helpful suggestions, and acts of kindness, these special people provided the encouragement we needed to face each day.

Although our paths to discovering new insights into caregiving varied, we both knew it was important to learn from those who had gone before us. The insights they offered on their successes and failures helped in smoothing out the bumps we encountered in our own journeys.

When you encounter occasional bumps and frustrations, they may seem overwhelming. You may even feel like you're being tested or stretched to your limits. The good news is that with the help of others and with strength provided by faith, you can meet those challenges. Place your trust in God to lead you through this journey. 2 Chronicles 20:12b says, "We do not know what to do, but our eyes are upon [God]." Therefore, live each day with your heart confident in God.

It may sound like a cliché to keep saying that "caregiving is a journey." However, in every conversation we had with both caregivers and those they were caring for, they all used the term "journey" in describing their experiences. They also emphasized that the journey is personal—and often unpredictable.

Your caregiving journey will be similar to any other journey. The more familiar and comfortable you are with your planned route and destination, the more confident you'll be moving forward. The less familiar you are with where you're headed and what you might encounter along the way, the more anxious and uncomfortable you'll be.

Since caregiving is personal, every caregiving journey will have its own unique and unexpected twists and turns. However, you'll discover that every caregiving journey follows a very predictable pattern that can be grouped into five distinct phases:

- **Recognition** – a time of awareness when you know care will be needed,
- **Reliance** – a time of involvement when the need to step up and be a caregiver becomes obvious,
- **Immersion** – a time when your presence and help become indispensable as your loved one desperately needs and depends on you,
- **Release** – a time of letting go when you recognize the end is near, and
- **Resource** – a time for sharing when you can reflect on your experiences and have the opportunity to help others in their journeys.

Although there is no way of knowing when each phase will begin or how long it will last, you can mentally prepare for the future by being aware of what may lie ahead. While there could be a period of months or even years as one phase blends into another, one thing is certain: each phase will bring its own challenges. No matter how your journey unfolds, continue learning and growing in your caregiving abilities while understanding and responding to your loved one's changing needs. By beginning and continuing your journey on a positive note, you should be able to look back and think, "I would willingly do it all over again."

Recognition: A Time of Awareness

Caring for someone who's an important part of your life might well be one of the biggest challenges you'll ever face. This can be especially true for married couples. When you made a life-long commitment to your spouse and said, "For better or worse, in sickness and in health," or something similar, you probably never imagined it would mean anything like this. Even family and friends can have similar feelings when they find themselves needing to step in and provide care on an up-close and personal level.

At first, when the prospect for providing care arose, both you and your loved one may have been in denial. You probably even thought that you wanted your lives to go back to normal again for as long as possible. You may have even thought, "Should we tell family members? Do we need to tell our friends? Surely this will pass," or even, "I can juggle my schedule for a month or two until this passes." However, when you enter the awareness and recognition phase, there is no denying the fact that you need to begin thinking about providing basic care.

In the beginning there may have been some early clues that life-changing events were occurring. Looking back, it may be hard to remember the exact sequence of events that took place as these changes became more noticeable. One day things were possible and then the next day they seemed to be unexpectedly challenging or difficult. Physical and behavioral changes that appeared to be out of the ordinary began unfolding. It may have even seemed surreal at the time these changes were happening, but you couldn't deny that things weren't the way they used to be.

You may have noticed a random stumble, a nagging cough, excessive tiredness, an unusual lump, moments of forgetfulness, an occasional slurred word, or a persistent ache or pain. Like most of us, you probably thought at the time that whatever was happening was unimportant and would pass on. However, whatever was happening persisted or became even more noticeable, eventually becoming a new normal rather than an oddity.

THE JOURNEY • 15

In what seemed like a time of uncertainty marked by notice-able physical changes, Gwen and I found our conversations in-creasingly turning to "what if" scenarios about how our future might unfold. It helped us to pray after these sometimes weighty discussions, both individually and together. We obviously prayed for healing, but we prayed for more.

We asked God for the peace of mind to face the changes that we knew were coming but found emotionally hard to grasp. The simple act of letting go and acknowledging the reality of the changes to come helped us turn our concerns and hopes over to God. Romans 12:12 reminded us to "be joyful in hope, patient in affliction, faithful in prayer." We took this advice to heart. Taking time to pray seemed to bring a sense of comfort in times of doubt and despair.

Reliance: A Time of Involvement

As the need for assistance grows, your loved one will eventu-ally move past the initial recognition phase and progress into the next phase of caregiving: reliance. In this phase you'll begin see-ing more and more changes in their need for care, as well as in your level of involvement in meeting those needs. There will also be noticeably increasing demands on your time and your emo-tional and physical energy.

In the reliance phase, at some level, the person you are caring for knows they need help. However, they may not be receptive to the idea of receiving help; they may even be defensive about accepting the help being offered. Reluctance on their part to ac-cept help may make your job as a caregiver more difficult. Don't take their apparent reluctance or defensiveness toward accepting help personally. You need to understand and accept the fact that their need for care and their looming loss of independence can be a very difficult time of transition.

Accepting the reality that help is needed can be an important crossover moment. It can be an extremely emotional, humbling, and scary time. Your loved one probably doesn't like the idea of beginning to feel helpless and vulnerable or feeling like they are becoming a burden. In fact, if they had the power to change the situation, they would probably like nothing more than to be completely independent again.

We heard a variety of statements from those being cared for that signaled when this moment arrived. For example, Catherine's mother often said things like, "Well, there are things I guess I can't do anymore," "Will you be here to help," "I need your help," and, "I hate to ask, but can you help me with this?" In response, Catherine would constantly strive to reassure her mother that she would be there for her. The same types of comments were true for me when caring for Gwen. As you think about these and similar statements, ask yourself if you've heard something similar and how it affected you.

These types of statements are all pointing to the realization that there are things your loved one has lost or is losing the ability to do. They can no longer independently manage everything on their own. They're becoming increasingly more dependent on you or someone else for assistance. Rather than stressing out as you add more caregiving duties to your already busy life, start thinking about the importance of finding a healthy balance between meeting your loved one's growing needs and your other responsibilities.

Immersion: A Time of Dependency

You'll know you've entered the immersion phase of caregiving when it starts to sink in that someone who is very near and dear to you is looking to you with a different set of expectations. For them, things just aren't the way they used to be and never will be again. They may or may not even know how to express what's happening to them. However, noticeable changes may be taking place in their expressions, body language, and even the look in their eyes. If you notice them wanting to express fears and concerns, be ready to sit down, listen, and discuss.

You can see them physically and literally beginning to reach out for help. They realize they are becoming increasingly dependent, yet they often want to remain as independent as possible. As the keystone caregiver your presence, assistance, love, and comfort become especially important. For me, this transition became poignantly obvious when Gwen recognized her growing dependency. We were sitting in the glider on the deck when out of nowhere, she looked at me and said, "It won't be long before you'll have to help me wipe my bottom."

When she said this, there was a slight quiver in her voice and tears in her eyes. Obviously, she had been thinking about this for a long time and finally had the courage to say it. I was stunned at first and at a loss for words. It was more than just a statement. It was a plea; a plea to discuss how the inevitable progression of her disease would impact our relationship. All I could do was look in her eyes, and then I finally said, "I love you and I'll do whatever it takes." This was the opening for a very long discussion. She leaned into me, and I wrapped my arm around her as we started coming to grips with some of the not-so-pleasant realities of how our future might unfold.

As you and your loved one progress into the immersion phase of caregiving, change becomes a constant part of your lives. This could be the point in your journey when you recognize that you're facing a new normal and that this new normal will always be one of change. These changes will require adjustments, flexibility, and adaptations for both of you. It should come as no surprise that changes brought on by intensifying dependency can be uncomfortable.

Things that your loved one typically could have done for themselves are now difficult or no longer even possible. Difficulties with simple tasks like buttoning a shirt or a blouse, putting on socks or tying shoes, or remembering names of family members start becoming obvious. For some caregivers, prompting or assisting with these tasks will be no big deal; it will come naturally. For other caregivers, it will be a more difficult transition; a transition requiring big adjustments and what may seem like radical changes.

Adjusting to these changes may take time as you begin tweaking your routines and learning how to grow into your new role as caregiving responsibilities become more intense. Meals will still need to be prepared and clothes will still need to be washed, dried, and folded. Children may still have to get to school on time and the house will still need to be cleaned. You may still have to get to work, and bills will still need to be paid. Medical appointments will still need to be made and kept. In addition, arrangements may need to be made and coordinated for assistance from family, friends, and possibly paid professionals.

You'll find yourself becoming totally immersed in planning for and meeting caregiving needs as your loved one loses more and more independence. You may find yourself becoming indispensable or needing to constantly be available to lend a helping hand. In the midst of what may seem like a never-ending rainstorm of demands, remember to keep your loved one involved as much as possible in their own self-care. Constantly be thinking about what you can do to preserve their remaining independence and dignity. Be aware of the fact that they are probably frustrated with the need for help and are grieving their loss of independence. They realize they're becoming totally dependent on you and others for assistance, and it can be upsetting.

Now is not the time for either of you to get stuck in the negative emotions of despair or wallow in self-pity. It's a time to evaluate your options and proactively plan for the future. Now more than ever before, you need to be there for them. Now is the time to move forward with positive energy and hope. Rely on God. He says, "I am the Lord your God who teaches you what is best for you, who directs you in the way you should go" (Isaiah 48:17).

Release: A Time of Letting Go

At some point you'll experience the fourth phase of caregiving: release. This will be a time of saying goodbye and letting go of your loved one. It will be a time when you experience deep sadness and the ultimate sense of loss. No one other than God knows when the end will come. It could be weeks, months, or years.

If you have questions about your faith, or you're spending time with someone who has questions about their faith, this could be an opportunity to have these questions answered. This is a time when life begins to slow down, and discussions can turn to deeper spiritual concerns. Consider reaching out to someone you know who lives out their faith and asking them to join you in these discussions. All of you can grow in your faith and experience God's love and reassuring presence.

This will also be a time for tears. Tears will come when you grasp the finality of events facing both you and your loved one. Although you might want to hold back these tears, don't. Tears can be a soothing release of emotions. Once you open up emotionally to these hard realities, it becomes easier to discuss personal feelings on a deeper level.

When Catherine's friend, Susan, confided in her that she realized she wouldn't be getting better, this verbal acknowledgment created a new level of understanding between the two of them. Catherine knew this was the time when she could move to a deeper level of caring by being there for her friend in any way she could. She began by simply holding Susan's hand every time they sat together as a source of comfort, expressing to her, "I am here with you." This led to reading Scripture, praying, and listening to worship music together.

If you've entered the release phase in faith and have planned for it, it can be a time of celebration. Even as difficult as preparing for separation may seem, know that it will only be temporary. Both of you can look forward to the time of celebration when you are reunited in heaven, where there will be no more pain, tears, or inabilities.

As an intentional caregiver, you have an opportunity to be a blessing for your loved one and to make each new day a time of celebration and hope. Know that God is with you as an ever-present help in this very difficult phase of your lives. Be reassured by knowing that "you have this hope as an anchor for the soul, firm and secure" (Hebrews 6:19).

Resource: A Time of Sharing

We firmly believe that caregiving is one of the most beautiful experiences you can share with someone very special to you in their time of great need. It can create a sacred bond that becomes a cherished memory that will always be a part of you. You will also have gained a great deal of knowledge and insight during this time. By the time you've finished your journey, you'll have an opportunity to become an invaluable resource. You can share what you have learned with others as they begin or continue their journeys.

Once people know that you've successfully negotiated caregiving challenges, they'll be drawn to you, wanting to know how you did it. They'll want the practical knowledge you've learned through your experiences to help them in their situation. This will also be a time to share, encourage, and remind them of the important role faith played in your journey. It was easy for me to tell others how Gwen and I confidently faced each day knowing that God was always with us no matter what was happening in our lives.

My friend, Don, who was caring for his wife, told me he always felt supported when I stopped by for a visit. He knew our journeys were similar. He knew I understood what he was going through and felt comfortable sharing his cares and concerns with me. When it was time to leave, I always asked if I could say a prayer for him and his wife. He always said yes. It was a blessing

for both of us knowing we could confidently share personal feelings and rely on each other. Our shared faith encouraged both
of us.

Catherine and I have had opportunities to rejoice with many
caregivers and their loved ones as they shared their stories with
us. We repeatedly heard from them how their trust and hope
in God sustained them. They were always ready to share their
favorite Bible verses and hymns that had served as sources of
encouragement.

Catherine's sister, whose twenty-one-year-old daughter was
dealing with terminal leukemia, was always quick to share what
verse or hymn God brought to her mind each day. She would
say, "This verse is perfect for me today," or, "The words to this
hymn are just what I needed to be reminded of God's faithfulness
and love." Through these simple acknowledgements, her sister's
heart was confident in God.

Faith, Your Sure Foundation

Your faith and reliance on God's presence will play a critical role
in the well-being of you and your loved one. It will also enhance
your effectiveness in being an intentional caregiver to know that
God is by your side. Isaiah 33:6 says, "God is the sure foundation
of your time, a rich store of salvation, wisdom and knowledge."
This simple but powerful truth has comforted so many in their
struggles with life-changing circumstances. Faith in God is the
foundation from which your strength, wisdom, and trust flow.

Faith also provides the assurance of hope and confidence
needed during uncertain times. Through faith, both of you can
find the emotional strength and encouragement needed to keep
moving forward. Knowing that God is with you will be an em-
powering force to sustain you each day. As you trust God to
guide you and help you, you'll be able to do things you didn't
even think were possible.

If you're part of a Christian faith community, embrace these brothers and sisters as they walk along beside you. Be prepared and willing to accept their offers of prayer, emotional support, and physical help as they're presented and extended. Their acts of love and care and their reminders that they are praying for both of you will be a source of great comfort. Trust God's promises that He will always be with you. Step out in faith and ask God to help you trust Him.

* * * * *

Pause for Prayer

It's our hope that you'll take the time to pause and pray often. Take some time alone each day to pray for patience, strength, and courage, both for yourself and the one you are caring for. Ask them to pray these same kinds of prayers, both for themselves as well as for you. Then take time together to pray those things that are on your hearts and minds. It's only through prayer that you'll be drawn closer to God.

Whether your prayers are softly spoken, boldly proclaimed, or tearfully uttered, God will hear them, as He cares for you. With this thought in mind, we will be asking you to "Pause for Prayer" at the end of each chapter.

> *Dear Lord, as we bring our cares and concerns to You, help us to exchange our worries and fears for trust and peace. May we have the confidence needed to handle the challenges before us as we trust You. Draw us close to You. Thank You that You are our strength and joy. Amen.*

CHAPTER TWO

Gaining Confidence

Pleasure in the job puts perfection in the work.
Aristotle

When you were young, you probably played a game called tag. When you were tagged, you were "it." Unfortunately, caregiving isn't a game, especially if you become the keystone caregiver. When Catherine, who was one of five siblings, recognized that her mother needed care, she realized she was going to be tagged "it." Although she was the next to the youngest, she was the one who was physically close at hand and willing to step up to the responsibilities.

If you're the one who's tagged "it," it can mark a noticeable tipping point, signaling significant changes ahead. There'll be questions about how you'll adjust to your new caregiving responsibilities. There'll also be questions about how the dynamics of this changing relationship will affect you and the person you are caring for, as well as other family members and friends. Even if you're not the keystone caregiver, you'll face similar questions when others depend on you to share the responsibilities of caregiving. How will you handle the demands that come with each new phase of caregiving? How will you gain the confidence of the person you are caring for that you will take care of their needs—and the confidence you need in order to be successful?

My daughter-in-law challenged my thinking about these questions when she said, "My dad would never take care of my mom the way you take care of Gwen. He could never do the personal things you do for her. He could never help her in the bathroom or with other personal needs because he wouldn't want to remember her that way." As I listened, my immediate thought was, "Sure he would." However, I didn't respond. How could I know what type of caregiver he might be? How will any of us know what type of caregivers we will be, or how we will respond, until the need arises?

When Catherine was finally tagged "it," she had to switch from working full-time to working part-time. Organizing her days became a necessity, not a nicety. She found herself needing to space out errands like getting her mother to doctor's appointments, grocery shopping for her, taking her to get haircuts, and making trips to the pharmacy. Rather than being overwhelmed, she used her prayer time to seek God's guidance and gain the confidence she needed to be an intentional caregiver. Throughout the day she turned to her favorite Bible verse, Psalm 32:8. It says, "I will instruct you and teach you in the way you should go. I will counsel you and watch over you." This promise gave Catherine the confidence she needed to lovingly take care of her mother.

Like Catherine, as you face these new responsibilities, take heart in knowing that there are many others who are currently dealing with similar situations who are both persevering and succeeding. They've embraced changes in their lives and are moving forward with positive attitudes. You, too, can gain this same level of confidence. God is bigger than any of your challenges and He wants you to remember His faithfulness and promises to always be with you. He will strengthen you and help you (Isaiah 41:10).

Plan for the Unexpected

Continue gaining confidence in your caregiving abilities by remaining flexible and learning to expect the unexpected. Learning to develop confidence while preparing to deal with these challenges will be a lot like learning to swim: lessons learned from watching experienced caregivers can help, but eventually you have to step in and try it.

When the physical or emotional challenges of caregiving start out slowly, you'll have time to plan ahead and learn the basics of how to cope with them. In situations where you find yourself dealing with the challenges of aging, noticeable behavioral changes, chronic illnesses, or the inevitable progression of a terminal disease, you have time to think about the future, adjust, and plan your next steps. Just like a beginning swimmer, you can practice and gain confidence as your skills progress.

However, in other situations there may be no time for contemplation and practice. When the need for caregiving happens suddenly, you don't have the luxury to calmly think and plan. You may have some of the same fears as a non-swimmer who is thrown into the deep end of the pool. You need to react quickly. You can either thrash around anxiously or try to keep your head above water; learning, adjusting, and reaching out for help.

As you begin to become comfortable with these new responsibilities, the demands may at times seem overwhelming. Experience is a wonderful teacher and confidence builder. However, you can never plan and be fully prepared for everything that comes your way. Things like unexpected excessive drooling, intense nausea, a severe bout of diarrhea, uncontrolled language, a sudden outburst of anger, or nodding off to sleep at inappropriate times, are just a few examples of what could be encountered. Many of these situations, and more, can happen when least expected and can be exceedingly awkward and potentially embarrassing.

So, be prepared to roll with the punches. There's no need to panic or be embarrassed by awkward situations. Even if you are stepping in from the outside to assist, deal with the issue at hand then shrug it off like it's no big deal. Don't worry if you make mistakes and don't beat yourself up with mental anguish when the unexpected happens. Dealing with awkward situations became easier for me as I practiced smiling and carrying on as if everything that was happening was normal. Improvising and adapting helps everyone around you feel comfortable.

Things that may seem like big things are really nothing more than small details that can be dealt with when taken in stride. A simple analogy about flying an airplane may help to highlight the importance of not worrying about big things; pilots learn early on that paying attention to small details is what really matters.

You may have never thought about flying an airplane, but it's possible to learn how to fly. Becoming a pilot takes skill: skill gained through training and practice to gain confidence. Much the same can be said about becoming a caregiver. It also takes skill: skill developed through training and practice to gain confidence. You can read about how to be a pilot or a caregiver, but both pilots and caregivers know that they gain the majority of their training on the job.

Flying may seem complicated and a bit daunting at first, but it isn't all that complex. It mostly involves hour after hour of following routine procedures that can occasionally be interrupted with a demanding challenge that requires quick thinking and responses. Surprisingly, caregiving is not that different. It involves hours and days of doing the same routines over and over again until faced with an occasionally difficult and sometimes stressful situation. Although it may seem like a crisis at the time, it really only requires occasional quick decisions and actions on your part.

For example, what would you do in some of these real-life situations? Say you come down with a really bad case of the flu and can't even take care of yourself, let alone someone else; or you get a call that your mother has fallen and has been taken to the hospital with a broken hip; or a storm caused a power outage, and you learn it could be days before power is restored; or, while cruising at an altitude of 35,000 feet and halfway to your destination, you suddenly remember you forgot to pack critical medications. Calmly finding solutions for these hopefully uncommon situations helps to build confidence in your ability to deal with the next unexpected situation.

Our friend, Amanda, told us about a traumatic incident she faced that caused intense anxiety.

> *While settling into the routine of caring for her husband after cancer surgery, she walked into the room where he was resting and discovered he had fallen out of his chair and was lying in a pool of blood. From that moment on until arriving at the ER, she truly was in a state of panic and fear! On the way out the door to the hospital, all she could remember was calling her pastor, who had been with them throughout his surgery and recovery. She was able to talk her through her anxiety on the phone and then was in the ER with her.*
>
> *The ER doctor quickly found the problem. The blood vessels inside her husband's colon had ruptured, filled, and then burst his ostomy bag. Their prayers were answered and the problem was solved, but she was still a nervous wreck. After getting him home from the hospital, she spent two months sleeping on the floor beside his bed in case it happened again. She was able to make it through this difficult time because she knew her pastor and church community were praying for them and she could feel the presence of God's protective hand.*

In any unexpected and potentially difficult situation, it's important to remember to breathe deep and stay calm. A quick prayer for peace, calm, and clear thinking can help to restore confidence in times of stress. No matter your circumstances, God is always there to give you the strength to persevere. Remember His promise found in Psalm 29:11: "The Lord gives strength to his people; the Lord blesses his people with peace." What other verses can you draw on in turbulent times for confidence, hope, and a sense of peace?

Understand the Challenges

As the keystone caregiver, you'll soon realize you're now in a situation where you're one person faced with the challenges of taking on multiple roles. These challenges involve serving the needs of two people while possibly meeting the demands of your job or taking care of children or grandchildren at the same time.

The responsibilities of caring for someone who has previously been independent can easily start to grow and become more demanding. You may find yourself taking on the additional responsibilities of becoming an assistant as well as a decision maker. It's only natural to be apprehensive and concerned about taking on these expanded responsibilities. Naturally occurring feelings of doubt and fear of failure aren't trivial ones to be brushed aside. It's okay to express these doubts and fears to friends, but also seek God's guidance. Expressing them openly and earnestly to God can be a time of trusting Him to give you the confidence needed in taking on so many new responsibilities.

As you begin functioning like a supportive assistant, you'll find yourself taking on an increasingly broader array of responsibilities. You'll start becoming more observant and sensitive to the changing needs of your loved one. You might even say that your "antenna" becomes more tuned in to their needs. This is a good thing. As Catherine settled into taking care of her mother, she started noticing important life-care details she needed to monitor. For example, she started looking in the refrigerator to see if food was being eaten, making sure medications were being taken, and checking the laundry basket to see if the clothes were being washed.

It'll be important to become flexible and comfortable with these new responsibilities. Some of them will be as easy as changing doses and timings of medications or monitoring oxygen, blood pressure, and glucose levels. Other responsibilities, such as providing comfort after chemotherapy treatments, changing dressings, giving shots, assisting at mealtimes, toileting routines, inserting catheters, or changing ostomy bags can be far more demanding. Adjusting to these new responsibilities will require changes to routines and a great deal of patience and understanding on the part of everyone involved.

There's also another important role faced by many caregivers: becoming the voice—the "interpreter"—for their loved one. As an interpreter, you may be placed in the position of trying to understand the spoken and often unspoken thoughts and needs of your loved one. In addition, you may also be called on to communicate these needs to others.

If communication becomes a problem, think about using low-tech as well as high-tech solutions to solve this problem. Gwen and I found several low-tech solutions as we worked together to meet our communication needs. For example, at home we used a sheet of paper with pictures indicating I'm hot, I'm cold, I'm thirsty, I'm tired, I need to go to the bathroom, I want to watch TV, I want to use the computer, and other common needs to simplify our communication needs. For more complex needs, an alphabet chart that let her spell out thoughts and needs took away the stress of trying to communicate orally.

We also adopted several high-tech communication solutions through the progression of Gwen's disease. She started out using an ergonomically designed keyboard and later moved to an eye-controlled mouse for emails and other computing activities.

When we were out with friends or in the car, she used a very small personal microphone that strapped around her waist with a headset to amplify her voice. These are just a few modifications we found useful in solving a problem while maintaining her dignity and allowing her to keep those all-important relationships with family and friends.

Catherine also discovered with one of her friends who was losing the ability to speak that using basic sign language words and phrases opened up new opportunities for communicating not only between them, but also other people. She subsequently introduced Gwen and me to American Sign Language (ASL). We invited several friends to join us as we learned. We couldn't help but laugh as we learned how to sign each other's names and thought of useful words and phrases to try out on each other. This experience opened up a powerful personal form of life-connecting communication.

One sign we all learned early on was how to communicate the need to go to the restroom. This need can be silently communicated by placing the tip of your thumb between the pointer finger and the middle finger while making a fist. This subtle sign can easily alleviate the awkwardness of a basic request no matter where you are. Finding one solution to a need led to other creative discoveries. Thinking about finding solutions rather than dwelling on problems helps to build your confidence in becoming an intentional caregiver. It also encourages the person you are caring for as they see you calmly dealing with challenging situations.

Learn to improvise, adapt, and overcome any challenge. Don't forget that every new challenge is an opportunity to lean on your faith. Ask God to help you accept these responsibilities and challenges with love, wisdom, grace, style, and of course, a sense of humor.

If you aren't already in the habit of reading a daily devotional like Our Daily Bread (ourdailybread.org), Jesus Calling (jesuscalling.com), Streams in the Desert (crosswalk.com), The Upper Room (upperroom.org), My Utmost for His Highest (ut-most.org), She Reads Truth (shereadstruth.com), or He Reads Truth (hereadstruth.com), etc., pick one or two and begin reading them. They'll provide you with inspiration, encouragement, comfort, and reminders that God is always with you.

Observe Others

Growing up, Catherine and I had the opportunity to witness many good caregiving role models in action: fathers, mothers, husbands, wives, relatives, and friends. These role models not only provided good examples to follow, but they also gave us the inspiration to be good caregivers.

Just the simple act of watching my mother care for others was inspiring. For example, I watched and helped my mother as she provided continuing care for a dear friend who was bedridden with rheumatoid arthritis and for an aunt who lived with us while fighting her losing battle with breast cancer. I also watched on multiple occasions as family, friends, and neighbors rallied around others in need with their thoughtful acts of kindness, prayers, and comforting support.

As Catherine often points out, watching her mother, who was a nurse, impacted her way of thinking and caring for others. In addition, watching the caregiver for one of her friends with Parkinson's disease gave her valuable insight, compassion, and training so that when it was her turn to care for another friend with the same disease, she was prepared to effortlessly step into the role. They may not have known it at the time, but these role models were a blessing as they helped to shape our approaches to caregiving.

Observing other peoples' caring actions and sincere dedication to serving others imprinted on both of us the positive benefits and blessings that flow from intentional caregiving. Seeing the responses of those they cared for and the joy they expressed for being able to help definitely influenced our caregiving styles. All of these experiences added up, providing us with an extra boost of confidence.

When it was my turn to care for Gwen, I knew I had a lot to learn, but I also felt like I had a solid foundation and was ready. If you've had the benefit of being around good caregiving role models, your caregiving learning curve will be much easier than it will be for those who missed out on these guiding examples. Remember though, no matter what level of experience you bring to the task, no one is an expert when they start.

Know Your Limits

Being an effective caregiver requires commitment. As you grow into your new responsibilities, your level of involvement and dedication to care will naturally influence your level of commitment. The more committed and intentional you become toward providing the best possible care, the more you'll be aware of your loved one's needs. Their needs will continue to expand, and the demands on your time will seem to be constantly growing. These expanding demands may at times seem to be in conflict with your needs, so remember to pace yourself and know your limits.

If you're still working or juggling family needs, outside assistance may be required. There may come a time, even with help, that you'll find yourself needing to relinquish some or all of these duties to others, but for now they're yours.

Think for a moment about what this may mean by reflecting on how it felt when you previously found yourself needing to care for someone who was sick with the flu or recovering from surgery. All of us, at some time or another, have probably been called on to do this. Were you comfortable taking on some basic caregiving tasks? Could you monitor medications, take temperatures, change the sheets, do the laundry, and fix easy-to-prepare meals? Or did you find even these tasks to be uncomfortable challenges?

If doing these tasks came naturally, you'll probably be able to ease into the role of caregiver. If you were daunted by trying to accomplish even basic tasks and found them to be uncomfortable or an imposition, you may find your new role to be more challenging and stressful than you think you can handle. If you found your friends or loved ones describing you as being oblivious or clueless to caregiving needs, you'll probably find yourself needing to rely on outside help to take care of even basic tasks.

This was true for our friend, Danny. As he struggled with the prospects of taking care of his mother, he knew he couldn't do it without a great deal of help. He could mow her yard, do her grocery shopping, and cook some basic meals. However, when it came to cleaning the house and bathing and dressing her, he needed help.

The same was also true for me. I could keep up with everyday tasks like cooking, doing the laundry, and washing dishes. However, I couldn't keep up with or didn't feel like cleaning the house. When I found myself struggling with this task, I quickly realized I needed help. Having someone come in every other week to clean the house was a welcome relief. So, don't feel obligated to do everything. Do those tasks that you can do and enjoy, and get help to relieve the burden of doing those things that you struggle with or don't enjoy.

Recognize You Can't Do It All

Whether on your own or with assistance, you'll discover that meeting the demands of caregiving requires a great deal of endurance on your part. To understand the importance of endurance in caregiving, imagine yourself in a race. This race isn't a sprint, but a long-distance race. Runners will tell you that toward the end of any long-distance race, fatigue becomes a constant companion. This is when runners, just like you as a caregiver, begin to question whether or not they have the strength and energy to continue.

It's important to watch for signs of fatigue and feelings of being overwhelmed. Like all caregivers, I experienced times when I thought I couldn't do it all. These feelings of being overwhelmed can happen to anyone, so there's no need to feel inadequate or ashamed. When one of Catherine's caregiving friends confided in her that she was feeling overwhelmed yet feeling guilty that she couldn't continue doing it all, they arranged for a substitute to fill in for a few days. Her friend was then able to get away and return, ready to carry on with her caregiving duties renewed and refreshed.

Rest assured that you can get through your struggles with confidence, realizing that "God gives strength to the weary and increases the power of the weak. Even youths grow tired and weary, and young men stumble and fall; but those who hope in the Lord will renew their strength. They will soar on wings like eagles, they will run and not grow weary, they will walk and not be faint" (Isaiah 40:29–31). God promises to provide strength, help, and comfort.

Reaching out for help may be easy for some and more difficult for others (like myself), but sooner or later everyone needs assistance. Gwen would often encourage me to "give over," which wasn't always easy. It meant letting go, asking for and willingly accepting help from others, for both physical needs and spiritual comforting.

The list of available services for both of you that can be found through churches, non-profit organizations, governmental agencies, and for-profit providers is both expansive and reassuring. Just knowing that assistance is available can be a real confidence booster.

If your friend or loved one is a veteran, contact the VA to learn more about the list of services available for those who have served in the military. Likewise, if your friend or loved one is dealing with issues related to aging, contact your local Area Agency on

Aging (AAA) for information on local services to meet some of their needs.

The following are ideas of the types of services you might want to access:

- Educational materials and lists of resources
- Companionship
- Running errands
- Meal preparation (Meals on Wheels)
- Grocery shopping (ordering online with delivery)
- Rides to appointments (ride sharing services like Uber and Lyft)
- Adult daycare services
- Bill paying or help with finances (only with a trusted person and with oversight)
- Housesitting
- Pet care (walking, grooming, and veterinary visits)
- Travel companions
- Lunch and dinner outings
- Memoir writing
- House cleaning
- Yard work
- Home organizing
- Bathing
- Laundry

These and many more services are there for your convenience, to ease your burden, and make life more enjoyable for both of you when it seems like there's just too much for one person to do. The professionals and volunteers in these organizations do their jobs because they care, because they truly want to relieve some of your burdens, and because they know you need help. They're prepared to provide or point you in the right direction to find the help you need.

As Catherine discovered when she was caring for her mother, different people helped in many ways. For example, a friend suggested she contact Meals on Wheels to relieve the necessity of cooking. A neighbor helped by taking out the garbage can. Another friend stepped in to mow the lawn. The newspaper always seemed to appear within easy reach next to the front door each morning. The mailman always knew her mother would be sitting by the front screen door, waiting for his arrival, and would actually hand the mail to her. These small gestures of kindness and help had a very positive impact on her mother and gave Catherine the confidence to know that reaching out for help was the right thing to do.

Almost everyone we talked to acknowledged the importance of knowing others were praying for them and their loved one. If you're not already being supported by a praying community, we encourage you to cultivate one. Reach out to family and friends, asking them to pray for both of you. Ask to have your names, cares, and concerns added to your church's prayer list.

When you do this, anticipate people asking what they can pray for. Have your prayer requests ready and share them when asked. Be as specific as possible. Be sure to thank them and let them know their prayers and love mean a great deal. As you accept these offers of prayer, emotional support, and physical help, never forget that "God is our [your] refuge and strength, an ever-present help in trouble" (Psalm 46:1).

* * * * *

Pause for Prayer

Dear Lord, I am filled with worries and concerns about what the future holds for us. Help me stay positive and be an encouraging caregiver. I need Your help to do my best. Please give me the strength and confidence I need to learn how to care for (my loved one). Help me plan for the unexpected and take on the challenges we face each day. Show us how to boldly reach out to others and accept their offers of support as we walk this journey. Thank You for Your promise that we are never alone and that You are always with us in the midst of our personal challenges. Please give both of us the patience, assurance, and guidance needed to confidently walk through each day. Thank You for Your faithfulness and love. Amen.

CHAPTER THREE

God Is with You

*The LORD himself goes before you and will be with
you; he will never leave you nor forsake you. Do not
be afraid; do not be discouraged.*
Deuteronomy 31:8

Have you ever been around parents caring for their special-needs child? If you have, you'll notice something different about them. The love and tenderness they show for their child is contagious. They always seem to have an inner peace.

Kay and Harry discovered soon after their healthy baby boy was born that something wasn't right. After multiple doctor visits and numerous tests, they learned that Ben would never walk and would be disabled for life. This was their baby, whom they had prayed for and were overjoyed to have. They knew now that they would be caring for him for the rest of their lives. But they also knew God had a plan in all of this and would always be with them.

Their constant love and tenderness for Ben was something everyone saw. Their lives radiated joy. How did they keep going day after day? You didn't have to talk with them very long before you realized it was their genuine faith that sustained them.

Even through the hard days, their confidence was in God who was their rock and gave them strength.

If you already have the peace Kay and Harry experienced that comes from trusting God, how can you deepen it? If you haven't experienced this level of inner peace and confidence, how can you gain it? Ask yourself, "When, where, and how can I strengthen and deepen my faith? Could God be calling me to live out my faith as a caregiver for someone I love?"

As I cared for Gwen, I often thought, "God has entrusted her to me." Rather than her being a burden, it was a blessing knowing that I could care for her. Recognizing this was God's call on my life, I knew I could trust Him to help me. Feeling the power of His presence in my life empowered me to do more than I could ever have expected to do on my own.

The same was true for Ginny when she was caring for her mother with Alzheimer's disease. When I asked her what role faith played in her caregiving, she leaned forward and passionately said, "There was no way my husband and I could have cared for my mom if it wasn't for our faith. We sat still with God and prayed at the beginning of every day. We asked for His guidance, comfort, and help with having patience and understanding how best to deal with mom." Then she added with a smile, "Any time we found a break in our days, we turned to God."

While I sat with Gwen after two hip replacement surgeries, I had plenty of time to think about how people needing care and those around them reacted differently as they struggled through rehabilitation. The same was true for their visitors. Some seemed agitated, depressed, resentful, angry, and often abusive toward everyone they encountered. Others were positive and hopeful.

It was obvious from both of these experiences that those patients and their caregivers who had a firm faith foundation trusted God to be with them. They were, in general, more hopeful and positive than those without that same foundation. People of faith always seemed to radiate an inner peace. Those lacking in faith seemed to be unsure about themselves and their futures, often brooding in anger and despair.

You can find the strength and encouragement needed to support both you and your loved one by leaning on your faith. As you reach out through prayer, find comfort in knowing God will be there with you every step of your journey.

Live Every Day in Awareness of God's Presence

Living every day in awareness of God's presence and knowing that He's always with you helps you to trust God and gain confidence in your ability to be an intentional caregiver. Joshua 1:9 reminds us to "be strong and courageous. Do not be afraid; do not be discouraged, for the Lord your God will be with you." This is a powerful and comforting thought to hold onto during your caregiving journey.

The Bible is full of God's promises to always be with you. Genesis 28:15 says, "I am with you and will watch over you wherever you go." Matthew 28:20 says, "I am with you always." All of these verses point to the fact that you can rest in the assurance that God is with you in this journey and will protect you, provide for you, lead you, and guide you. Are there other verses that speak to you?

It's important to remember that no one knows as much about your life, your circumstances, your loved one, and the solutions needed more than God. So, begin with God as you start each day. Let go of your fears and anxieties by asking Him to direct your thoughts and steps. Learn to recognize and live with the awareness of God's presence every day. He is there for you.

Focus on Spiritual Practices

Spiritual practices will strengthen your faith as you connect with God. These practices will provide comfort, support, and encouragement along your journey. The question, then, is how do you cultivate spiritual practices? The answer lies in consciously devoting personal time on a regular basis to focusing your attention on God. It's been said that if you do something regularly for at least thirty days, it will become a habit. So, set aside some time every day when you can quietly sit in God's presence and practice being with Him.

Discovering spiritual practices can lead to a more Spirit-filled life. This may seem difficult at first. However, with a little patience, time, and experience, you'll soon discover that these practices can become a natural part of your life. Let's take a look at some of them:

- Practicing God's Presence – having a continual awareness of God's presence
- Rest – slowing down
- Silence – resting from noise
- Solitude – resting from people
- Prayer – talking to, worshiping, and seeking God
- Sabbath Keeping – setting apart one day a week for rest and worship of God
- Meditation – reading God's word for reflection and interaction with God
- Bible Study – knowing what the Bible says
- Worship – honoring and adoring God
- Service – helping, caring, and sharing God's love in the world
- Confession – admitting weaknesses and faults to God
- Simplicity – uncluttering your life to focus on what really matters
- Self-Care – nurturing and taking care of your body, mind, and spirit

For a more complete list and further thoughts on how to engage in additional spiritual practices, we recommend reading

Adele Calhoun's *Spiritual Disciplines Handbook* and Richard Foster's *Celebration of Discipline.*

Explore and Realize the Benefits

The idea of beginning to explore one or two of these practices can easily begin the process of connecting you with God. It's a way to create space for God to speak, lead, and guide you. If you're so busy trying to handle caregiving duties while trying to juggle all the other demands in your life, you won't be able to hear God or even be aware of Him trying to help you.

Be sure to make time (and not feel guilty about taking time) for this to happen. For your own peace of mind, it's important to make a deliberate effort to slow down and rest in God's presence. Resting in God's presence strengthens and equips you to face the challenges that lie before you each day. It's a time of turning your heart and mind toward God. It's a time of slowing down, of hearing—and paying attention to—God's voice.

You may be thinking, "My hands are so full with caregiving and taking care of myself and everything else that needs to be done each day; there's no way I can find time to rest in God's presence." If this is what you're thinking, reevaluate your day and find at least a few spare minutes to focus your attention on God. If you find yourself being interrupted with caregiving duties, don't get discouraged or give up.

Ask yourself where and when there might be a break with time to find a few quiet moments. Is there time for a few quiet moments in the morning before your loved one wakes up, or when they take a nap? Is there time to find a few quiet moments when they're getting ready to go to bed or after they go to bed? Is there time to find a few quiet moments when you're in the shower? Is there time to find a few quiet moments when . . . (you fill in the blank)?

Even if your quiet moments are brief or hard to find, use them to sit quietly: just you and God. Don't feel guilty if this is not an extended amount of time. It's okay to start with short amounts of time whenever you can find them. It will be easier to go from there and carve out longer blocks of dedicated time later on. Taking intentional time away from your daily routines and demands will become a welcomed break and eventually a habit.

The importance of these practices and quiet moments with God came to light when Melanie shared the following story. When her mom had a stroke, she was shocked. Her mom was only seventy-two and had been healthy all her life. Her parents lived in Florida, but she lived in North Carolina. At the time she had ten- and eleven-year-old-sons, her husband was a pilot, they owned a business, and she was writing and serving with a ministry. Saying that she was busy would be an understatement. But now she felt the need to add into her schedule a long-distance trip to Florida every two months to spend time with her parents. There would be many times when she thought to herself, "There is no way I can do all this."

> *I knew the only way I could prevent falling apart during this time period was to lean on God. I didn't have a lot of time, so I used time on flights to and from Florida to pray. I said breath prayers throughout the day when with my parents. I chose to use the spiritual practices of simplicity and self-care while focusing on my priorities and giving my time and energy to those things. That meant saying no to many other people and things pulling at me! I tried to read the daily devotion in Jesus Calling each day, as these were short but powerful readings.*

Perhaps, like Melanie, you may unexpectedly find more moments of quiet times scattered throughout the day. Look for these moments and purposely use them to be still and focus on God. It will certainly be beneficial for both you and your loved one.

Don't worry about making a mistake or trying to be perfect as you begin to rest in God's presence. Find a spot where you can be quiet and alone as you explore these practices. Settle into your comfy spot. It could be on your couch, in your favorite chair, or . . . (you fill in the blank). Then, breathe deeply and sit still.

As you relax and turn to God, learn to freely express your heart and speak openly to Him. Use a breath prayer or short phrase to focus your attention and help you be still. Some people call them "arrow prayers." Words and phrases like "Here I am, God," "Calm my heart," "Help me, God," or "Show me what to do next" are all you need to say as you get started. Talk to God just as you would to your best friend. Tell Him what's on your heart; what you're thinking and feeling. Over time, you'll find your mind being refreshed and your strength renewed. You'll feel God's peace and sense Him leading you.

Don't be concerned if your mind wanders during your prayer time; it happens to all of us. Your life is busy and as hard as you may try, it can be difficult to shut out this busyness. Just as you would in any conversation, refocus on the purpose of your prayer, knowing that God will understand your distraction given everything you are going through.

It may also help to be conscious of some sights and sounds that can serve as reminders of God's presence. Some examples of these reminders are butterflies, clouds, a type of bird, heart shapes, a special color, the sound of ringing chimes, a screen saver image, or some other sight, sound, taste, texture, or fragrance that is meaningful to you. I started out looking for doves and then moved on to English sparrows before finally settling on butterflies as my reminder.

It seemed like everywhere I looked, I saw a butterfly or an image of a butterfly, and it reminded me that God is with me. Catherine uses butterflies, too, but she also likes the color yellow and the sound of ringing chimes. She is delighted when she sees and hears them. Also, when you hear a song or one comes to

mind during the day, pay attention to it. Could the song be a reminder of God's presence in your life? Any of these little things,
things you see and hear every day, can serve as triggers, reminding you of God's presence and that He is with you.

Once Catherine started using the color yellow to remind her
that God was with her, she was excited to discover how powerful
the reminder was when first going to visit someone whom she
knew needed comforting. As she tentatively drove down their
long street, she saw that every single driveway had a yellow recy-
cling bin. This filled her with the courage she needed to make the
visit as it was a visual reminder that God was indeed with her.

As you explore and realize the benefits of these spiritual practices, be sure to encourage your loved one to practice them, too.
This could be a time for sharing with each other how you hear
God speaking to you and reminding you of His love. What a
blessing this will be for both of you.

If you don't already have a Bible app, consider download-
ing one for reading and listening. A quick search for answers to
questions or words of comfort, inspiration, and hope can then
be as close as your fingertips. Putting your favorite Bible verses
on index cards for regular reading can also bring comfort and
reassurance. Having them written out can make them easy to
visualize when you need reminders of God's strength, peace, and
presence. Reflecting on and remembering these Bible verses will
remind you that you aren't alone. It was always a special treat
when visitors thought about adding one of their favorite verses
to Gwen's growing stack.

Ask Hard Questions
Sitting still with God each day also provides opportunities for
the quiet, reflective time needed to name and speak hard questions. One hard question that seems to come to the mind of everyone who faces the challenges of caregiving or being cared for

is "Why?" This troubling one-word question eventually leads to even more questions: Why me? Why us? Why now?

Questions of Why may lie unspoken or be voiced plaintively by you or the one you are caring for. These Why questions are like the proverbial elephant in the room: try as you might to ignore them, you can't. They're too personal and important, and they just won't go away. Sooner or later, you have to deal with them. Why not now?

Failing to ask these questions, seeking clarity, or listening for answers can lead to feelings of abandonment, anger, grief, distress, and despair. These questions may be voiced as simple inquiries or expressed as angry demands for answers. In one voice or another, you're sure to ask other age-old questions, like "Why does God let bad things happen to good people like us?" or "Why does He allow bad things to happen to people who believe in Him?" In addition, you may also ask Him for insights into other disturbing questions, like "How can I bear this pain and suffering," "How can I deal with this uncertainty," or "How can I continue?" These are questions that need to be acknowledged, so don't be afraid to ask them.

As you wait for answers, will you live in hope, anger, doubt, uncertainty, or hopelessness? How you deal with and seek answers to these types of questions will set the tone for the dynamics of how your caregiving relationship will develop. It sets the stage for dealing with future unforeseen problems and unanswerable questions. You may even try to answer your own questions by thinking, "Surely if I have enough faith and fervently pray, healing will come!"

No matter how hard you pray, answers may never come. All you need to do is read the book of Job in the Bible and you'll see that even one of God's most faithful servants never got answers to why he always seemed to suffer through sorrow and loss. Just like with Job, remember that no matter your circumstances, the outcome is always in God's hands. Although we try to be in control, we can't be in control. Don't miss out on the life you have now while looking for something that is out of your control. Only God is in control, and He wants us to trust Him. Proverbs 3:5–6 reminds us to "trust in the Lord with all your heart and lean not on your own understanding; in all your ways acknowledge him, and he will make your paths straight."

Yes, miracles do happen! Prayers for healing were answered for one of our friends. This vibrant, thirty-something, athletic woman was doing everything a health-conscious person should do. Then, seemingly out of the blue, she was diagnosed with stage-four breast cancer and given little hope for survival. Everyone who knew her said it made no sense and asked why this had happened to her.

While this question haunted her and those supporting her, she bravely battled through experimental treatments as well as multiple surgeries, radiation, and chemotherapy treatments. All through this journey of treatments, fears, doubts, and concerns, her husband, two young children, extended family, and friends were always there for her. In her case, prayers were answered, and her cancer is in remission.

She commented many times that there was no way she could have persevered and survived this grueling journey without the support and prayers of those who were close to her. In addition, during times of doubt, she was comforted in knowing there was a whole host of "prayer warriors" whom she knew were there with her in spirit or who physically pitched in to lend a helping hand to her and her family. While she didn't know what the future held, knowing that God was with her and people were praying for her gave her the encouragement, comfort, and hope she needed.

There's nothing wrong in praying for a miracle because they do happen. But simply praying for a miracle is not enough. Don't set yourself up to only be disappointed if a miracle doesn't happen. We've walked beside many people who fervently prayed for a miracle, never to see it happen. Simply praying for a miracle is too limiting. Don't let troubles shake your faith; let them shape and strengthen it. Look back and remember those times when God has helped you and protected you in the past. He's still with you and will answer your prayers in His own way and in His own time.

Trust in God's Faithfulness

God's love for you is constant. He knows everything you and your loved one are thinking and feeling. He knows your fears and concerns and is there to comfort and guide you. The opening quotation in this chapter, from Deuteronomy 31:8, says it all: God goes before you and will always be with you. Can you take this thought to heart and be as calm and confident as Kay and Harry? Can you put your trust in God and rely on Him to give you the same level of peace they experienced? Are you aware of His goodness and faithfulness?

Once you begin opening your minds and hearts to accepting His comfort and peace, you, too, can experience their same level of joy. Just as they did, place your trust in God to guide you as you rely on Him throughout your caregiving journey. Watch for times when you can see Him working in your lives. Notice how is He helping you and giving you strength, guidance, and peace.

No matter how uncertain your future may appear, you and your loved one can begin each day on a positive note by simply thanking God for the gift of a new day. Start each day by thanking God for being with you and trusting Him to guide you through the day. As you continue to grow in your faith, trust God for healing, guidance, and understanding. As you calm your heart, consider offering the prayer Gwen often used. It goes something like this:

> *Dear Lord, thank You for today. You have blessed us in so many ways and we are grateful. Be with us*

today and help us feel Your presence. Keep us by Your side. Thank You that You know our circumstances. Continue to guide us and show us the way forward. We ask for healing (you can insert your specific situation/request here), yet we know that You know best and that we can put our trust in You. We surrender to Your will. Amen.

As we come to the close of this chapter, sit back and reflect on where you have seen God working in your life. Take time to encourage each other as you both continue developing your spiritual practices. Begin listening to and sensing how God might be guiding you. Be patient and remember that He wants you to look to Him for your strength and joy. Take comfort in knowing that He is always with you. May He calm your heart, helping you to trust in His faithfulness.

* * * * *

Pause for Prayer

Let's do something a little different at the end of this chapter. Take some time to sit quietly in silence and solitude. Begin to let the stresses and worries of the day slowly melt away. Reflect on how you have experienced God's faithfulness during the day. Now, think about those cares and concerns that are the most personal for you and your loved one (it may help to write these down). Then breathe in deeply, exhale slowly, and begin talking to God just as you would in any conversation. Start by simply saying,

Dear Lord, thank You for Your faithfulness and for always being with us. There are so many things that weigh on our minds: (voice your cares and concerns). Please help us to be conscious of Your presence as You walk along beside us and give me strength to do my best to be a loving caregiver. Amen.

CHAPTER FOUR

It's a Partnership

No road is long with good company.
Turkish proverb

Almost everyone who spent time with Gwen and me commented on the fact that we always seemed to be working together and enjoying ourselves even in difficult situations. They were right! We were always working together, solving problems, and doing everything possible to remain positive. As we encountered challenges, we learned how to overcome them by working together as a team. We were in sync with each other. Working together as partners made things go much smoother. We also knew that God was with us, helping us handle the challenges we encountered.

Think about your caregiving relationship. Would you describe yourself as being a nurturer or a martyr? In other words, do you find that caregiving comes naturally to you, or do you find caregiving to be a difficult obligation to be endured? Or, maybe you would describe yourself as falling somewhere in between these two extremes.

How would you describe the person you are caring for? Are they appreciative of your efforts, or are they stubborn, resistive, and grumpy toward most everything you try to do to help? In other words, do you find them being positive and accepting toward your efforts, or do they seem to be acting like an uncooperative curmudgeon, always finding something to complain about? Or would you describe them as falling somewhere in between these two extremes?

The dynamics of caregiving will definitely change relationships and create new interpersonal dynamics. How you both deal with these changing dynamics will set the stage for the effectiveness of your caregiving partnership. When you genuinely want to provide care and your loved one wants to be cared for and graciously accepts your caregiving efforts, your partnership will flourish. Ecclesiastes 4:9–10 says that "two are better than one . . . if either of them falls down, one can help the other up." This is such a great reminder of how two people working together can help each other succeed.

However, just knowing the importance of cultivating a partnership is one thing. Knowing how to create and nurture that partnership is something else. Do you want to develop a positive caregiving partnership? If so, then ask yourself, "How can I make this happen?"

Let's start answering this question by focusing on the two most important people in a caregiving partnership: you and the person you are caring for. You're in a position to encourage the well-being of your loved one. Your loved one in turn can cooperate by remaining as self-sufficient as possible and being receptive to your help. Although partnerships can be formed with many others (extended family members, friends, neighbors, etc.), for now we're only looking at the importance of your two-way partnership. We'll explore multi-party partnerships in the next chapter.

Caregiving Is Personal
When a partnership is formed, it should be for the benefit of both parties. When you become partners, you agree to be there

for each other and cooperate with each other on a very personal level. If either one of you enters into this relationship with a selfish attitude such that it will be all give on one side or all take on the other side, you might as well structure your caregiving arrangement like a business transaction.

You could approach caregiving like a business relationship, thinking of it as an obligation and simply hire different people to take care of your loved one's needs. However, choosing a businesslike approach can result in a relationship devoid of love and the benefits found in personal commitments. You'd miss out on the blessing of walking the journey with someone you deeply care about. Intentional caregivers don't just wait and hope for good things to happen, they actively seek to make things better.

If you're reading this book, we know you're seeking to nurture a positive relationship and want to be actively involved and do your best to be a successful caregiver. So, let's look at a few situations that are reflective of two-way caring partnerships. These examples provide some insights into how partnerships form and function. As you read and think about them, you'll begin to get an idea of how the dynamics of a caring partnership might work.

Let's start by looking at a very basic example and then move on to other, more complex examples. Think for a moment about a favorite plant. Do you have a relationship with that plant? Is it a caring relationship? If your plant is alive, you have established at least a basic caring relationship. How did this relationship develop? It began, and continues, by you watering and fertilizing your plant and maybe pruning or repotting it on occasion. Maybe you even talk to it, trying to coax it to grow or bloom. These are all conscious actions on your part. If you didn't care for it, it would wither away and die.

Now let's take a look at another caring relationship that's more complex: the partnership we develop with our pets. It's a known fact that cats, dogs, birds, and many other pets bring a great deal of joy to anyone in need of comfort and companionship. When you take on the responsibility of having a pet, you know it will need your care and attention. How does a relationship develop into a partnership that has the potential to bring so much joy?

Your pet knows it can depend on you to take care of its basic needs: food, water, and cleanliness. Your pet depends on you, and you in return, are blessed with its loyalty and comforting presence. I know that our dog, Sprocket, and our two chattering parakeets, Mama and Papa, brought continual joy and hours of entertainment and companionship to Gwen.

"Okay," you might say, "I get the idea of the positive benefits that flow from a beneficial give-and-take relationship. However, the relationship between someone in need of my care and these examples just doesn't seem to be the same. I'm facing a completely different situation, one dealing with a wide range of human emotions."

Your loved one can talk back, get their feelings hurt, feel sad, be angry, be frustrated, smile, laugh, express appreciation, and show love, just to name a few of these emotions. So, how can these fairly easily understood analogies about plants and pets be applied to your far more complex caregiving relationship? How can you deal with these emotions and move from simply maintaining a relationship to nurturing it into a beneficial partnership?

A good starting point for nurturing a beneficial partnership is to be encouraging with your words and actions. Words give life to our feelings and emotions, but we also know that actions speak louder than words! 1 Thessalonians 5:11 tells us to "encourage one another and build each other up." Nourish your partnership by choosing words that give life, hope, and support. Ask for God's direction and nudges on how to choose appropriate words, and then how to convey their meaning to your loved one.

Your choice of words, sincere efforts of inclusion, physical demonstrations of care, comforting acts, and presence are natural ways of nurturing a personal caring relationship. As you strive to nurture this relationship, you'll begin seeing your loved one respond in a positive manner. They'll be able to relax and thrive knowing you deeply care. You'll both be blessed with a growing and flourishing partnership.

Working Together

Continue strengthening your partnership by consciously making every attempt to involve and encourage your loved one's participation in as many everyday activities as possible. As you communicate expectations and plans, ask them if they have suggestions for how both of you can do things better together. Always listen and be prepared to act on these suggestions and express your appreciation and thankfulness by acknowledging their cooperation and help.

Sometimes finding a solution to an unmet need is as easy as having a conversation about it. When Gwen started using her walker, she commented several times about how inconvenient it was for her to carry things to her desk or chair. After hearing these frustrating comments a few times, I finally asked, "What kind of things would you like to carry?" She was quick with an answer: "My Kindle, my cell phone, a cup of coffee, or a snack."

This got me to thinking and making suggestions for different types of "baskets" that might work. Gwen finally came up with the idea of using a plastic shoe box and I had the idea of fastening it to her walker with plastic zip ties. It was a perfect partnership solution: the shoe box rested on the walker crossbar and the zip ties held it firmly in place. This proved to be an easy solution that yielded positive results for many years.

Rather than assuming that what you're doing is creating the supportive relationship you desire, ask if what you're doing is helpful. By continually seeking input and involvement you'll find those things that are truly meaningful and helpful. This will create feelings of accomplishment and enjoyment.

Finding ways to actively include the person you are caring for in the caregiving process isn't all that difficult. You can consciously seek their help and suggestions in accomplishing useful tasks. Consider having them do easily performed activities like putting dishes into and taking them out of the dishwasher, sorting and folding clothes, stacking underwear, or matching socks. When dealing with younger children who are part of the family, include them in these types of activities and also have them help with chores like setting the table or playing with siblings. They could also help by cleaning up and organizing toys after playing, or by reading to siblings or visitors.

Activities that are centered on food almost always create multiple opportunities for involvement. Everything from menu planning and making grocery lists to preparing and mixing ingredients for baking and cooking are tasks that can be enjoyed by everyone. Even something as simple as putting together a salad can create a sense of working together and of accomplishment. The list of things you can do to involve your loved one in everyday activities is only limited by your imagination and creativity.

While you may consider grocery shopping to be a chore, to someone else it may seem like an adventure filled with new experiences. A trip to the grocery store not only serves as an outing but can also provide a time to be involved together in completing a meaningful task. One caregiver related how helpful it was to take her mother along with her to the grocery store when she did her shopping. Since she had to get her own groceries anyway, this created a win-win situation. While they walked through the store together, she'd give her mother a shopping cart and let her pick out the things she wanted to buy. This gave her mother a sense of teamwork.

Continue fostering the personal aspects of your caregiving partnership by intentionally involving your loved one in the give and take of everyday care decisions. Consider finding opportunities that will encourage and support their dignity. Seemingly simple things like letting your loved one select what they want to wear can demonstrate a desire to be inclusive and supportive.

Assisting with little touches to enhance their appearance also promotes a sense of self-worth that can be uplifting for both of you. Doing things like helping to neatly comb or style hair, helping with a touch of makeup, or helping with a shave are easy ways to boost self-esteem. When you have pride in their appearance, they'll know it and show it.

Basic life functions like eating and toileting can often become more problematic as diseases and debilitating conditions progress. For example, when eating becomes difficult, using a clothes protector (bib) and ergonomically designed eating utensils and dishes can be easy adaptations for boosting independence and confidence. There's no need to make these adaptations conspicuous; you can easily carry needed supplies and adaptive aids in your pockets, purse, or backpack. Our daughter-in-law noticed this need and created a special pack that fit on the back of Gwen's wheelchair, complete with her name in embroidery. It carried everything we needed for outings, including snacks, and when people noticed her name it served as a great conversation starter.

There may be awkward times, though, when you're dealing with very personal and what many would consider to be private and intimate needs. This becomes very obvious when wives deal with their husbands, husbands deal with their wives, sons deal with their mothers, daughters deal with their fathers, etc. Even if you can't help or are extremely uncomfortable in dealing with awkward situations because of differences in relationships (gender, physical size, or age differences), never forget that your loved one is depending on you. While working together to find solutions, remember your loved one finds comfort in knowing you're willing to help in overcoming these challenges and maintaining their dignity, and are never far away.

Developing Compassion
Anticipate your loved one's needs as you continue to patiently encourage independence on their part. At the same time, attempt

to develop a deeper level of empathy for their needs and feelings. This may be easy to say, but it is nevertheless a difficult skill to cultivate. Having empathy requires focusing on understanding another person on a personal level. It means learning their needs and desires and then developing the insights to meet them.

Look up the definition of empathy, and you'll see something like this: empathy is understanding, sharing, and even experiencing the feelings of another person, ultimately resulting in an intellectual or emotional identification with that person. Why is the ability to develop a sense of empathy so important as a caregiver?

Developing a sense of empathy is important because it encourages you to imagine what your loved one is thinking and feeling. This can be done by paying very close attention to not only their words, but also their actions and reactions. Making the extra effort to pay this level of attention causes you to slow down, pause, and think about what's best for your loved one. This is a helpful step in beginning to sense their feelings of dependency and frustration.

You may already think you know someone on a personal level, especially if you've known or lived with them for years. However, remember that they're now in a different situation, one of needing care while continuing to lose their independence. Truly knowing them requires developing a deeper level of insight. You'll need to sincerely attempt to understand how they feel and what they want and need to make their life as enjoyable as possible. Don't forget that they may no longer be able to do—or they have great difficulty doing—many things they previously did for themselves. They've become increasingly dependent on you and others to meet some or all of their needs.

Being placed in a situation of depending on someone else isn't a good feeling. To get a taste of how this loss of independence might feel, try struggling with some everyday basic tasks. For example, try signing your name with your nondominant hand.

Or put on a pair of thick, oversized gloves and then try putting on a pair of socks and shoes and tying the laces. With these gloves still on, try performing a simple task like threading a needle. Or try putting on a blindfold and attempt to open a can of soup, heat it, and eat it. If you feel awkward trying to accomplish any of these tasks, just imagine what it must feel like for your loved one who faces similar challenges every day.

To get a feeling of being even more dependent, sit down in a wheelchair and have someone push you through a store. You've seen those wheelchairs by the front doors of many stores. All you have to do is try it once, and you'll quickly discover what it feels like to put yourself in someone else's shoes who has no other choice but to accept this type of assistance. Observe how others look at you, think about how they perceive you, and notice how they react as they see you being pushed through the store.

It may help you gain an even deeper understanding of the importance of empathy by thinking back to a time when you were in need of help. Do you remember a time when you had the flu or really severe intestinal problems and had a difficult time trying to raise your head up out of bed or struggled to get to the bathroom in time? Or how about a time when you broke a bone and needed someone to help with a basic life function like scratching an itch or reaching for something that was just out of your grasp?

Can you remember how you felt when you depended on others in these or other similar situations? You may have been looking for sympathy, but you what you really wanted was help, understanding, and patience. By remembering your feelings in these times of need, you can begin to appreciate the importance of developing empathy and the impact it can have on your relationship with your loved one.

When empathy for someone else's needs develops into a higher level of understanding, you begin to have compassion. As you gain compassion, you become even more intentional in your actions. You literally desire to suffer with them and take actions to reduce their discomfort or suffering. Being compassionate doesn't require doing big things, it requires doing the little things that add up to make a big difference. You'll find yourself becoming way more effective and efficient when you're in tune with your loved one's needs.

We've all heard that a person's eyes provide a "window into their soul." In becoming compassionate, you'll find yourself looking into your loved one's eyes, searching for a deeper understanding of their needs. You'll discover that their eyes speak volumes of information and can provide invaluable insights into their emotions. As you look into their eyes and concentrate on everything they say, listen intently while paying close attention to their body language. With this level of focused attention, you'll have the opportunity to understand and respond to their innermost feelings and needs.

The more compassionate you become, the more confident you'll be in your ability to meet your friend or loved one's needs. Ephesians 6:7 says to "serve one another wholeheartedly, as if serving the Lord." Being compassionate is a wholehearted way of intentionally serving others.

Dealing with Unwanted Challenges

No matter how good the relationship, unwanted challenges can create barriers to effective partnerships. For example, consider how you and the person you are caring for might approach the following common situations: your efforts to help are rejected or go unnoticed, your loved one should no longer drive, or you have no choice but to move your loved one into a care facility.

In the first situation where help is needed, your loved one might be resistant to accepting any help. In fact, they may even be resentful, unwilling, or hostile toward your efforts. You may be facing this type of challenge if you notice any of the following negative behaviors on the part of your loved one:

- Are they dismissive?
- Are they rough and abrupt?
- Are they demanding?
- Are they demeaning or abusive to you or other caregivers?
- Is their language crude and unfiltered?
- Do they have a "don't give a hoot" attitude?
- Do they act like it's all about them?

If any of these behaviors sound familiar, ask yourself some thought provoking and introspective questions. Is it the way I am approaching the situation? Am I creating or fueling the problem? Could I change my behavior? Does the person I am caring for appear to be acting out, trying to convey a message of, "When will this situation change?" Are they showing frustration by expressing the thought, "When will I get better?" or "When will I not need your help anymore?" You may not find satisfactory answers to these questions. These behaviors may be a reflection of their personal struggles and have nothing to do with you.

So, what can you do to support your partnership? First, when faced with negative behaviors, step back and try to relax. Then seek guidance through prayer. As you pray for guidance and especially patience, ask whose behavior needs to change: yours or theirs? Second, go to someone you trust. Freely unburden your cares, concerns, and frustrations on them. Ask them the same types of questions and be open to the answers you receive.

Finally, you may want to reach out for professional help (doctors, nurses, counselors, therapists, pastors, social workers, etc.), voicing your concerns and processing what's happening or has happened. This can often help in bringing clarity to the events you've experienced and give you the strength to persevere and move forward.

Tamara is a good example of a caregiver who experienced this type of behavioral challenge with her brother, Roger. The situation she found herself in began to spiral out of control when

Roger didn't get his way. She was able to call him out, bringing it to his attention that his behavior was inappropriate and unproductive.

Instead of being transferred to the VA hospital where there were no available beds, Roger was transferred to a local nursing facility for rehab after one of his many diabetes-related surgeries. He wanted to be back in the familiar surroundings of the VA hospital, where he'd always gone for care after surgery. When he was told this wasn't possible, the frustration became too much, and he became verbally abusive with his sister and the nursing staff. He finally began settling down when Tamara was able to calmly remind him that his behavior was disrespectful, inappropriate, and would do nothing to change the situation.

Tamara needed to remember they were in a partnership, so she didn't want to be argumentative, talk down to Roger, or sound like a parent scolding a child. She knew how important it was to speak with truth and love in this situation and remind him that "we are in this together." Being honest like this with your loved one requires a delicate balance. While it may help to diffuse anger and frustration in many situations, we recognize that when dealing with someone suffering from Alzheimer's and other forms of dementia, this probably won't be a workable possibility.

Something else that can be just as stressful on even the most loving partnership is when you know the person you are caring for should no longer be driving. The loss of this privilege can be traumatic for both of you. It's just one more major life event signaling a further loss of independence. However, allowing someone to drive whom you know is a danger to themselves or others creates legal liabilities for both you and them, and therefore must be addressed.

Some drivers recognize when they need to relinquish their keys while others stubbornly resist. If your loved one is resistant, don't try to continue this conversation alone. Enlist the help of other family members, friends, or medical professionals. If you try to press the subject on your own, you could place undue stress on your relationship and forever be the bad guy who took away their freedom. If these discussions don't work, you can anonymously contact the Department of Motor Vehicles and they'll make an assessment of whether or not a license should be revoked.

Finally, you may be faced with the more difficult and painful choice of finding a care facility when the challenges of caregiving become more than you can handle even with outside help. If you've been discussing this possibility, the need may become obvious to both of you. However, don't consider this as one of your first alternatives.

Before making this deeply emotional decision, diligently seek solutions that will allow the person you are caring for to remain in familiar surroundings. We've both seen caregivers who've given up way too early or too easily, seeking institutionalization as a solution to coping with challenging behaviors or the demands of caregiving. Many of these individuals have shared their regrets with us as they've looked back and wished they'd explored other options. However, if your loved one becomes uncooperative or unresponsive, or you can no longer physically meet their needs, you may have no other choice but to find some type of specialized care facility.

Setting Boundaries

Even in a supportive caregiving partnership, establishing boundaries is essential to nurturing a healthy relationship. In the immersion phase, this will be even more important as the demands on your time become more complicated. If you begin setting simple boundaries early, then it becomes easier to establish more challenging ones later on. At this point you might be thinking, "What are boundaries, and why are they important?"

Boundaries are protections you establish to safeguard your time and emotions. Think about a typical caregiving scenario that emphasizes the importance of setting boundaries. You're at work or running errands and your loved one is at home. Remember, you have obligations and time constraints on your day, but your loved one's day typically doesn't have these same constraints. They're sitting at home with time on their hands, even if someone is staying with them.

They may think nothing about texting or calling you when they want something or think of something they would like to say or ask. They know you are willing to help, so why not reach out when a need comes to mind. Let's say, for example, they decide they want some chocolate ice cream. This is a simple request and one that you can easily take care of on the way home. However, when you get that same call or text two or three times in a thirty-minute time span, it starts to become annoying.

To keep this from happening and to keep you from becoming frustrated, you'll need to agree upon and set boundaries on when and how you'll communicate while apart from each other. When you've established the fact that your caregiving relationship is a partnership, creating boundaries should be a fairly straightforward task. Once you've established boundaries, you can adjust them as your circumstances change.

However, we recognize that boundaries may be difficult to enforce (as much as you would like to) when you're dealing with someone who is suffering from Alzheimer's disease and other forms of dementia. You'll probably find yourself facing the difficult reality of becoming more like a parent caring for a child as these types of diseases progress.

You can begin setting boundaries by maintaining control of your time and doing things as much as possible on your schedule, not on a schedule that is dictated or creates demands that are imposed on you. Always search for ways to be proactive by lovingly setting and controlling these boundaries. Mealtimes, medication times, and bedtimes are easy to establish and are good starting points for creating consistency.

You may also need to encourage your loved one to help you in setting boundaries. We talked to one caregiver who said her husband had so many people coming by to help that the helpers ended up being a problem. Her husband was too polite to decline their visits and offers of help. This influx of people and calls became more of a burden than a help. She ended up having to let her husband know that he had to put reasonable limits on the number of visits and calls he received. While establishing boundaries, do it together and keep reaching for God, trusting Him to guide you and show you the way (Psalm 25:4–5).

Having a Grateful Heart

When both you and your loved one focus on being thankful with grateful hearts, there will be many benefits that flow through your caregiving partnership. Openly share and remember to say how thankful you are for each other. Practicing gratitude can be energizing, lead to feelings of joy, and promote a zest for life. Having grateful hearts encourages you, lightens your burdens and concerns, creates times for smiles and laughter, and helps you appreciate each other. Gratitude provides the optimism needed to face the journey together.

Gratitude takes the focus off of your concerns and places them on God. It brings you closer to Him and helps you keep a positive, thankful attitude. If you're having a hard time being grateful, taking time to recognize God's blessings can give you a renewed outlook to appreciate His love, peace, and presence. Prayers of gratitude open your hearts, allowing you to see God's goodness all around you. It helps you notice and appreciate God working in your lives. Learn to be joyful, to be thankful, and to pray continuously (1 Thessalonians 5:16–17).

Gratitude doesn't always come naturally, so make a commitment to be grateful every day. Begin or end each day by finding things in your life that you're grateful for and share them with each other. You can start by being thankful for little things like a sunny day or soft gentle rain. Then stretch your awareness and thinking. Focus on being thankful for things that bring joy to your caregiving partnership. We know one caregiver who keeps a list of what she is grateful for, adding one new thing to her list each day. Acknowledging these blessings becomes a daily reminder of God's faithfulness to her and her loved one. Thank God for His goodness and His promise to always be with you.

* * * * *

Pause for Prayer

Dear Lord, thank You for being with us in this journey and for what we are learning as we grow together. Thank You for the reminder that we are in a partnership supported by Your love. I am so thankful for (my loved one) and that we can be here together for each other. Open my eyes and heart to be more compassionate in seeing my loved one's needs. Help me to keep a positive, thankful attitude. Help us to recognize the blessings You send us each day. Amen.

CHAPTER FIVE

Be the Team Captain

*I am still determined to be cheerful and happy, in
whatever situation I may be; for I have also learned
from experience that the greater part of our happiness or misery depends upon our dispositions, and
not upon our circumstances.*
Martha Washington

You never know whom you'll meet in the grocery store.
This day it was Kelly. Our conversation started out like
any other between two casual friends passing each other in the aisles. "Hi, it's good to see you. I haven't seen you in
a while. How are things going?" I didn't know at the time that
she was helping to care for her grandmother, but our conversation ended up being the perfect description of how a care team
should work.

She opened up, telling me she'd been spending most of her
free time with her eighty-five-year-old, semi-independent
grandmother. Her grandmother had been having some kidney
problems, but things were starting to look better. Seeing that she
wanted to talk, I pushed my grocery cart to the side and settled
in to listen.

It seemed that things began improving when her family found a specialist who was very familiar with her grandmother's condition. This was the first ray of hope in what had been a bleak situation. Kelly went on to talk about how blessed they had been that so many people had stepped in to help care for her grandmother. She described how her parents, brother, friends, neighbors, and church members rallied around her grandmother. She told me how they helped by taking her grandmother to long-distance doctor appointments, reaching out with phone calls, stopping by for visits, bringing an occasional meal, sending cards and emails, and constantly reassuring her that they were praying for her. There was no question in Kelly's mind that if they hadn't come together to support her grandmother, she'd be on dialysis and no longer living on her own. Maybe it hadn't been planned, but they had come together as a care team.

What I heard reflects the blessings both Catherine and I have witnessed and experienced when caring and supportive people— your care team—are there to help. When all the pieces fit together with medical professionals, family, and friends working together as a unit, your journey becomes more enjoyable. The combination of these people along with your faith community will provide the strength and encouragement that comes from knowing you aren't alone.

As your supportive care team members come together, surrounding you with their love, you have a unique opportunity to coordinate these relationships. The question is, how do you go about nurturing these relationships to enhance your caregiving efforts? How do you know who should be on your team? How do you go about bringing them together and working with them as a team? How can you become the team captain?

Your Care Support Pool

When you finally realize you can't take care of everything yourself, how do you decide who can help? As the team captain, you have the opportunity to decide who becomes a part of your care support team and what level of involvement they'll have on your team.

The decision-making process about who to include will be a whole lot easier if you approach it systematically. No matter how large this potential pool eventually becomes, just as Kelly discovered with her grandmother, there are some who'll be more essential than others. For her grandmother, it was a very special and caring doctor. Then there was her son and daughter-in-law, who put in the extra effort to arrange for additional support and care visits.

In the process of finding people who will be the right fit, remember that God is there to guide you and nudge you to recognize who those people are. Pray for God's guidance in forming your team. We saw God working in Susan's life after she was diagnosed with Parkinson's disease. Complications from her illness led to her needing more help with everyday chores like shopping, cleaning, laundry, and cooking.

She looked to God for guidance and enthusiastically described how her prayers were answered. Her daughter stepped in to coordinate the schedule of friends and helpers by keeping a calendar on the kitchen counter. She would write in the names of people who were able to help at specific times and on specific days. This visual method served as a basis for organizing her mother's care team. As more help was needed, it was easy to add to the schedule. It became an enjoyable way for everyone on the team to see how they fit into the overall caregiving plan.

As you think about your potential support team and what it might look like, try this simple demonstration. Drop a pebble into a pool of water. You and your loved one are represented by this pebble. The pool of water represents all of the people who could join your team, as well as those with whom you'll simply cross paths during your journey.

Once the pebble hits the water, notice what begins to happen. From that one small initial splash, ever-growing circles begin rippling outward. For some, these circles may be few and small, while for others they may be large and numerous. The circles closest to the point where the pebble splashes into the water are smaller in size but are more pronounced than the larger outer circles of subsiding ripples.

The size and intensity of these ripples are similar to the impact different individuals will have in your lives. Those close-in ripples represent people who'll have a much greater impact than those found in the more distant, subsiding ripples. Putting names to each of these circles of people provides clarity to how you think about everyone in your potential pool of caregiving support. Placing names on the circles also provides an easy way of grouping people and thinking about how they might enhance your caregiving team.

Care Team Partners

As you think about the people you see and interact with on any given day, can you visualize how they might fit into your caregiving team? As the team captain, placing people into common groupings serves as a form of mental shorthand, creating easy-to-visualize practical categories. In our conversations with caregivers, we found it helpful to use the following groupings:

- The **Core** – you and your loved one
- Your **Vitals** – individuals who are essential care team members
- Your **Constants** – individuals who are always accessible and available to help when needed
- Your **Reachables** – individuals who are truly concerned and could potentially help if needed

Making these distinctions helps you focus your attention on everyone who is available to help while identifying any gaps that may exist in your support team. Once you've decided who fits where, you can then decide how much time and emotional energy to expend on initiating, nurturing, and growing these relationships. Classifying people as vitals and constants lets you know whom you can depend on to always be there for you. Identifying others as reachables provides a sense of comfort, reminding you that they can be called on when needed.

It's important to remember that the people in each circle may change, possibly moving from one group to another and in and out of your life as your journey continues. Things can also change in people's lives, making them no longer able to help. So, be open to change. Embrace new people who offer their help while celebrating the contributions of those who are no longer available or able to help.

Close-In Support

The first and most noticeable ripple surrounding the spot where you dropped the pebble in the water represents those individuals who are the closest to you and your loved one and who are available to provide the most support. You'll find yourself relying on this very near and dear, close-knit circle of people to provide many necessary support functions. Since they know both of you so well, their support is invaluable. They can often read your thoughts and feelings, and they just seem to always be there to listen and ask thought-provoking questions. They are available to openly discuss your needs and concerns—and, when needed, to just listen.

You can think of those in this closest circle as being your rock-solid supporters, many of whom you may also consider to be partners in your caregiving efforts. These are your vitals, who you know will always be there for you and whom you can comfortably lean on for support. They truly know you and your loved one and will earnestly seek to help you, pray for you, and do everything they can to support and comfort both of you. You will find that their support and friendship refresh your soul (Proverbs 27:9 TLB).

These vitals will demonstrate empathy, and at times compassion. You'll feel safe sharing your innermost concerns, hopes, fears, and frustrations with them. The ability to freely share or vent whatever is on your mind, even your whiny complaining thoughts, is important for keeping yourself in a good state of emotional balance. Sharing your frustrations and concerns can help you refocus your attention on your loved one.

Sharing personal information with your vital(s) might seem difficult at first, but stepping out in trust will help you mentally process the changes both you and your loved one are seeing and experiencing. They are there for you. As they listen, they can ask questions that will hopefully make you stop and think, helping you see beyond the busyness of your days. They're there to listen, not to solve your problems, although they can often provide helpful suggestions; they're not as emotionally involved or facing the same daily challenges that are occupying your time both physically and mentally.

Don't be afraid to share the basics about your loved one's condition and your concerns and frustrations with your vitals. If they're going to walk beside you and support you in this journey, they need to know the troubles you and your loved one are facing. Keeping what's troubling you a mystery or private doesn't do any of you any good. In fact, the simple act of sharing these details with someone you trust can be incredibly liberating.

Vitals are so important that we've noticed many situations in which one of them ends up eventually becoming a caregiver to the caregiver. This can definitely be a blessing, but it isn't something the caregiver can plan; it just happens. The natural way vitals have of just showing up and stepping into this role at the most opportune times becomes a much-needed source of comfort and encouragement. They can also recognize your needs and step in, helping you delegate basic caregiving tasks to other team members.

You might find it helpful to enlist the services of one of your vitals as a co-captain on your caregiving team. You may also find this person taking on the all-important role of being a personal confidant. It may take some searching and trial-and-error to find this person, but it'll be worth your time. You'll be looking for someone who is non-judgmental and who can hold your conversations in confidence.

Another group of people who'll be members of your vitals circle will be your team of medical professionals. There's no question that your loved one will need more than one doctor and that you'll need to develop a special working relationship with each of them. The titles for these doctors may vary depending on where you live and how expansive the medical community is. They'll go by many different names, but there may be an internist, family doctor, primary care doctor, or general practitioner.

Whatever they're called, they'll look after your loved one's general health, serving as a focal point for their overall medical care. They can and should assist in coordinating the care provided by any needed specialists. All of these doctors will become an integral part of your care team. In addition, some of these doctors will often provide more than just medical care.

Our family doctor was an invaluable resource and member of our care team. He was always observing both Gwen and me for signs of change. When he saw a change or sensed a need through our conversations or body language, he was quick to ask questions and offer helpful advice. He was able to point us in the right direction to get more information and suggest possible referrals.

Carefully select and cultivate medical professionals as they are added to your care team. You can overlook a gruff bedside manner, but don't tolerate a doctor or medical professional that doesn't get to know your loved one and their needs, concerns, fears, and frustrations on a personal level.

A good starting point for finding specialists is by asking for referrals. Don't just ask other doctors. Ask people who are dealing with the same diagnosis as your loved one for their recommendations of doctors and other medical professionals. Cast a wide net in your searches for these specialists, including any chiropractors, nutritionists, therapists (occupational, physical, and speech), etc., that may be needed along the way.

Don't just settle for the first name you hear or the easiest appointment you can schedule. You need to find the best, so search for the best within your budget, schedule, and physical travel time constraints. You may have to travel across town or even to another town to find the right match. For us, the critical turning point in Gwen's care was that all-important trip to the Mayo Clinic.

As you meet and add new medical professionals to your care team, think about your initial visits as being similar to a job interview or a first date. These initial visits and interviews should be a time of exploration and getting to know each other. First, you want to find doctors who are specifically trained and current in their specialties. Next, you want to find doctors with whom both you and your loved one can relate. I always asked Gwen the same basic questions after our initial visits. "Did you like the doctor? Did you feel comfortable with the doctor? Would you like to see this doctor again? Do you trust this doctor with your care?" I also asked the same questions before any medical professional became part of our care team.

Both Catherine and I have talked with many caretakers who were too shy or intimidated by medical professionals to make a change when needed. If you don't think your needs are being met or your questions are being adequately answered, or you don't connect with someone on your medical care team, find someone new. "Breaking up" isn't all that difficult. Simply thank them for their time and keep looking. If it isn't a good relationship, don't stay in it.

Each situation will be different, but having the sense of being respected and effectively cared for and trusting the person in charge of medical needs is reassuring. With this level of confidence, you can deal with the sometimes-differing opinions expressed among doctors, family, friends, and other care team members.

Available Support

The next and still larger outer circle of people in your care support team will be your constants. This group includes extended family, friends, and relatives who truly know and care about you and your loved one. They can provide every imaginable kind of support, be available when needed, and do a whole host of little things that can make a big difference. Picking up groceries or prescriptions, bringing by a meal, or offering a ride to an appointment may seem like little things to them. However, these helpful gestures can lift an enormous burden off your shoulders, especially when you're struggling just to meet everyday challenges.

Another group of people who are still important, but whom you'll find in an even more distant outer circle, are your reachables. They will interact with you on a fairly regular basis but aren't intimately involved with you or knowledgeable about the details of your caregiving situation.

They can be found at work, in clubs and organizations, support groups, your church family, or neighbors. Since they are less involved and aren't with either of you on a continuing basis, you shouldn't expect to receive their constant support or assistance. They may be willing and able to respond when needed, especially if asked, but they aren't close enough to your situation to anticipate or to know when or even how to respond to your immediate needs.

There will also be people outside your caregiving circles with whom you only occasionally interact. They may feel a sense of obligation to interact and ask something polite like, "How are things going?" or, "Is there anything I can do for you?" When asked these types of questions, a simple reply like, "Thanks for asking, things are going as well as can be expected," is all you need to say. Keeping your responses positive is important as you never know when these casual inquiries may turn into more meaningful involvement. You can encourage these connections and show appreciation for their interest by asking them, "Please keep us in your prayers," or simply saying, "We appreciate your prayers."

Be an Engaged Advocate

Even though you may sometimes feel like you're just a chauffeur tagging along to appointments, one of your roles as the team captain is being an engaged advocate. Becoming an engaged advocate goes a long way toward ensuring that proper care and attention is being given to your loved one's needs and concerns. Be alert in every appointment but be especially alert to your medical team's actions and their attention to details. When dealing with any professional service provider's office, especially over the phone, if you're not getting the answers you need, don't give up. Ask to speak to a nurse or keep working up the chain of command for answers. Don't be shy about calling back or asking to speak to a supervisor.

When dealing with medical professionals, be knowledgeable about what they are doing and why. You can do this in the following ways:

- Prepare a list of concerns to talk about before each visit
- Have notes or a journal detailing changes in your loved one's health
- Take a list of medications and dosages to every appointment

- Ask questions for understanding and clarification, while actively listening
- Record or document your visits for later review
- Remain open-minded and do not become judgmental

We all need and depend on doctors for our care, but don't become unconditionally enamored with them. Just because someone has a "Dr." in front of their name it doesn't mean they know everything, and they may not be as in tune to your loved one's needs as you are. Don't automatically take "no" or "there's nothing that can be done" as answers to your questions. Seek more insight by asking, "Why?" Medical visits should be a dialogue, not a monologue. Be assertive and seek a second opinion when necessary, ensuring your loved one receives quality medical care.

Make sure you have the doctor's (or any medical professional's) full attention during each visit. Don't forget that they are busy people with many things on their minds and they are working on very tight schedules. If they are focused on making entries into their mobile device, it's okay to wait until you have their full, undivided attention before asking your questions. Be informed about medical options and discuss these options with your loved one. Decide together as a team what's best for your particular situation.

As you learn more about medical services, you'll begin developing a newfound level of comfort in your discussions with these providers. However, simply learning medical terms and jargon won't be enough. Along the way, you'll need to:

- Be ever vigilant and attentive to everything that is happening in your lives
- Manage your emotions, so you can manage your loved one's care
- Gain experience that can only come through trial and error

- Maintain an optimistic outlook on life that empowers you to solve problems and excel

Recognize that God wants to be intimately involved in every part of your lives. He promises to provide what you need each day, so prayerfully ask God for the wisdom needed to make important caregiving choices. James 1:5 says, "If any of you lacks wisdom, he should ask God, who gives generously to all." Make this a time for trusting God to lead and guide you, unfolding the way before you. Anytime you're facing an uncertain situation, reach out in prayer. Pray for clarity and calmness. In addition, think about committing the familiar Serenity Prayer composed by Reinhold Niebuhr to memory. It goes like this: "God, grant me the serenity to accept the things I cannot change; courage to change the things I can; and wisdom to know the difference."

Don't Be Surprised

As diseases progress and physical changes occur, some friends you considered to be part of your caregiving circles will disappear. They just seem to evaporate for no apparent reason.

Both Catherine and I have been heartbroken as we watched long-time friends slowly fade away. We learned over time that a lot of people are often uncomfortable with any type of adversity and find themselves at a loss for what to say or how to interact. Be aware that this might happen and don't be surprised.

So many physical changes can happen that are out of your control. For example, losing hair after cancer treatments, being confined to a wheelchair, or having slurred speech after a stroke can make someone look and feel different. This often creates awkward social interactions. With some diseases like Alzheimer's, Lou Gehrig's, multiple sclerosis, Parkinson's, or other debilitating neurological conditions, we have seen people react as if the person may even be contagious.

These conditions won't go away quickly or even go away at all. In fact, they may become more pronounced over time. So, how will you react when your loved one is treated differently? When it comes to your vitals, you probably won't even need to think about this question. They'll take these changes in stride. However, with casual acquaintances and the general public there can be awkward situations, very noticeable stares, and odd reactions.

Don't dwell on the fact that your loved one may be treated differently and that friends may fade away; instead lean on those who are there to support you. Recognize that people often struggle and find it very difficult to be around a person who is physically challenged or has a disease or illness with which they are unfamiliar. Don't be surprised or take it personally. Acknowledge what's happening and talk to your loved one about these hopefully unintentional slights. Learn to accept the situation in which you find yourselves and continue doing those things that bring you and your loved one enjoyment. Draw on your faith by leaning on God as a true friend who will never desert you. God assures you that He is by your side, that you will never be alone, and that He holds you by the hand, promising to help you (Isaiah 41:13).

Encourage Connections

Don't dismiss the people who begin to fade away or who are uncomfortable and don't know what to say. Remind them that their presence is comforting and helpful. Encourage them to keep in touch by sending cards, making brief visits, emailing, instant messaging, and texting. Let them know this makes a huge difference.

They can also be made to feel more comfortable if your interactions with your loved one are matter of fact and light-hearted. What you may not realize as you make adaptations and go about what you consider everyday activities is that others are watching your actions. When you're comfortable, it makes them feel comfortable. It creates opportunities for them to ask what they can do to help or how they can best interact. Be ready with suggestions. Be a role model they can emulate. You, better than anyone else, know the little things that can serve as bridges to keep relationships alive.

When one of our friends began having difficulty speaking, we noticed that many of her friends stopped coming to see her. Some of those who began staying away commented on how hard it was to be around her. This was when Catherine had the idea of inviting two or three of them to visit on the same day she was visiting. She recognized the importance of coordinating these visits so she could facilitate open and ongoing communications. All sorts of topics of interest shared in these times together created an atmosphere of inclusion and love. These visits eventually became opportunities for a variety of shared activities like watching special movies on TV followed by a time for prayer at the end of each visit.

We've also noticed loved ones withdrawing from connecting with friends and family over the phone due to their hearing loss problems. This shouldn't happen to anyone, as voice-amplified and voice-to-text devices are available at no charge for those who've been diagnosed with hearing loss. That's right—it won't cost you a penny, so ask your phone provider or doctor to have this type of equipment installed!

As my friend Kelly realized, caregiving is easier when many people come together to serve in different supporting roles. As the team captain you'll be initiating, fostering, and maintaining these connections. This will be relatively easy to accomplish with people who are in your close circles of support. All it takes is picking up the phone, texting, and using social media to stay connected. If using technology is uncomfortable, you could ask one of your vitals to assist in setting up a group messaging format to keep others updated or to communicate special needs.

Now, thinking about everything you've read in this chapter and about your loved one's needs, prayerfully consider filling in the following blanks with names and contact information. You may not have names to put in each category at this time, but at least give it a try. If you have trouble thinking of a name to fill in a blank, think about how you might find someone who could fill that gap and grow your circles of support deeper and wider. Reach out and ask. You might be surprised at how big your care team can be and how many people are available to help.

The Core (You and Your Loved one)

_____ _____

Team Captain

_____

Team Co-Captain

_____

Your Vitals

_____ _____

_____ _____

_____   _____

Your Constants

_____   _____

_____   _____

_____   _____

_____   _____

Your Reachables

_____   _____

_____   _____

_____   _____

_____   _____

_____   _____

_____   _____

* * * * *

Pause for Prayer

Dear Lord, as I move into the role of team captain, help me to be a good communicator and to remain positive. Help us to recognize the people You are bringing into our lives to walk along beside us. Help us to keep trusting You as You lead, guide, and provide for what we need each day. Thank You for Your constant love and care. Amen.

CHAPTER SIX

Make a Meaningful Difference

Too often we underestimate the power of a touch, a smile, a kind word, a listening ear, an honest compliment, or the smallest act of caring, all of which have the potential to turn a life around.
Leo Buscaglia

It was sharing time at our caregivers' support group, and Patrice was visibly distressed. Tears began running down her cheeks when it was her turn to share. When she finally found her voice, she blurted out through a muffled sob, "I just can't do it anymore." After listening to her frustrations, we began asking questions. All of her answers seemed to point to the same conclusion. Damian, her once fairly independent husband, was losing more and more of his physical capabilities. She was compensating for this decline by stepping in and taking over for him.

Patrice was losing patience with his fumbling and slowness and wanted things to be the way they used to be. She missed going to the movies, eating out, and spending time with friends. We couldn't solve her problems, but we encouraged her to be patient with Damian. We also told her how important it was to keep up as many normal routines as possible and to let him keep trying to do things for himself, no matter how tedious or difficult a task might appear.

The meeting ended on a positive and hopeful note as we shared techniques that we'd found helpful when encouraging our loved ones. This meeting wasn't sponsored by a church group, so it was heartwarming to see the majority of the group gathering around Patrice after the meeting and offering to pray for her and keep her in their prayers. Several meetings later, she thanked us for listening to her in her time of distress. She was grateful for the way we offered support and suggestions. It helped her re-think how she and Damian might be able to work through their frustrations and improve their situation.

Rather than facing a situation like Patrice, start thinking now about what you can do to be a more intentional caregiver. Ask yourself, "How can I enhance my loved one's journey? What can I do to make each day more meaningful and fulfilling?" As you think about your responses to these questions, ask God to nudge you and show you ideas that can enhance your caregiving style. Remember that He is there to lead and guide you (Exodus 15:13).

Lay the Groundwork

A beautiful summer garden full of blooming flowers that last all season doesn't just happen. It takes planning, preparation, and hard work. It takes all of these same things to lay the groundwork for an intentional caregiving relationship. Once this groundwork is in place, you can begin considering opportunities for adding extra flourishes.

How will you know if you're at least satisfying your loved one's essential needs? How will you know if you're creating an enriching environment? The answers to these questions can be found by talking about them with your loved one. As you inten-tionally involve your loved one in these discussions, you'll begin experiencing the blessings that flow from making shared deci-sions and doing more together. It will become easier to share with each other what you're feeling. You'll both find yourselves beginning to relax while feeling loved and understood.

In addition to learning and practicing caregiving basics, encourage your loved one to talk about their desires, expectations, and dreams. This is also a time for you to openly share your feelings on the same topics. Don't assume your loved one understands your feelings and frustrations or that they have lost interest in things they used to do. Through your discussions, you may learn that it has become more difficult for them to go out to eat, go to a movie, or do other things that seemed so common in the past. If these are things either of you would still like to do, discuss how you can make it happen.

With discussion, planning, preparation, and a few adaptations, most previously enjoyed activities can still be enjoyable experiences. The changes you make will not only strengthen and enhance your caregiving partnership, but they will also increase the confidence both of you need to continue working together as a team.

Once you start gaining confidence in providing the essentials of care and comfort, start thinking about doing more. It could be something as simple as trying out a new recipe or being a bit more adventuresome—for instance, encouraging the exploration of a new hobby. Once again, ask your loved one for their ideas. When you find something that's enjoyable, stick to it, but always remain flexible and willing to try something new.

While some caregiving needs will be fairly easy to address when your loved one can still lend a helping hand, others will be more difficult. Tasks like bathing, dressing, eating, and toileting can become more challenging as your loved one's strength, dexterity, and mobility ebb away. Even things that once seemed as effortless as brushing teeth and getting ready for bed (including repositioning in bed), as well as assistance with walking and transfers, can eventually become significant challenges. Helping with these tasks when it becomes a necessity builds your confidence and encourages your loved one.

Enhance Your Efforts

As you strengthen your caregiving foundation, begin thinking about opportunities you have to make a positive difference in your loved one's life rather than focusing on the obstacles you face. Be open to opportunities to enhance your caregiving efforts by continuing to encourage your loved one's input and seeking the advice and help of others. Ask your vitals these two questions: "If you were in my shoes, what would you do to make my loved one's life more comfortable?" and, "If you were my loved one, what else could I do differently?"

When you hear their answers, ask yourself, "Am I willing to give at least some of these suggestions a try?" If you're willing to try, then do it. If you aren't comfortable with trying something new, ask your loved one for their input on how you can do it together. Observing others doing the same thing may also be helpful. In addition, it may be more than the two of you can handle, so ask for help. When our friend Susan could no longer shampoo her hair, her husband asked Catherine to come over and shampoo it in the sink. With the blow drying added in, the task turned into fun and laughter and became something to look forward to each week.

While thinking about opportunities to encourage your loved one, consider how you can include those who are willing to step in and help. This could also become a time for sharing faith stories and examples of God's daily blessings. I can still remember one of Gwen's occasional fill-in caregivers. She would always arrive with a story about what had recently happened in her life. These were stories about how the sink got clogged, how the dog got out, or how a plant she had never noticed was now in full bloom.

She was always thankful and full of joy, telling us how God had orchestrated the sink being fixed, the dog being rescued, and her recognition of the beautiful flower He had created just for her. Her life was so enriched by her faith that we, too, were touched by her joy. We couldn't help but laugh at her stories and smile at the blessings she found from God in everyday events. Her stories reminded us of God's faithfulness in all our lives. These shared stories added a ray of sunshine to our lives every time she joined us.

Broaden Your Thinking

As you become comfortable taking care of basic caregiving needs, start thinking about what you can do to step up your efforts. This means going above and beyond simply thinking, "These are the same old routines I have to do every day." Think back to that beautiful summer garden full of blooming flowers. The groundwork for this beauty took planning, preparation, and hard work. It also took good soil, plenty of water, sunlight, and warmth for it to flourish. Likewise, a successful caregiving relationship depends on taking care of the basics, but there are other things needed for it to flourish: **perception**, **patience**, **passion**, and **possibilities**.

Since you've already been working on developing empathy, perception should come naturally. Through perception, begin thinking about how you'll approach each day from the perspective of your loved one's wants and needs. Ask yourself questions like, "What do I see that my loved one would need help with? What can I do to brighten each day?"

By asking these types of questions and thinking about your answers, your caregiving style will naturally evolve. Consciously continuing to do little things to improve everyday routines can brighten any day. For me this was easy. I knew Gwen loved fresh-cut flowers, a made-up bed every morning, specialty coffees and teas, and snuggly blankets while watching TV. If you have trouble thinking of new things to do on your own, this would be a good time to have a discussion with one of your vitals. They know you, and more importantly, they know your loved one, so encourage them to make suggestions.

You'll also need patience when stepping up to the next level of providing intentional care, and your loved one will need to learn to be patient with you as you do so. In fact, you'll both probably need more patience than either of you ever thought possible! This became obvious for Patrice as she tried to do everything for Damian rather than waiting on him to complete these tasks. She found that practicing patience wasn't easy, but she learned that it was important for Damian to feel independent by doing things on his own for as long as possible.

You know that you can get dressed faster, put on your socks and shoes faster, eat faster, move around, and do anything, in general, faster and with greater ease than your loved one. This will also be true for anyone stepping in to help. So, remind yourself, and caution anyone stepping in to help, to avoid the natural tendency to take over and speed things up.

As your loved one begins to lose physical or mental abilities, it would be easier and less demanding to do some of these cumbersome tasks for them. But doing things for them that they can still do for themselves will only lead to something called learned helplessness. Learned helplessness can easily occur as your loved one starts giving up and letting you do a task rather than struggling through to complete it on their own. The potential for this to happen is especially likely as you move through the reliance phase and into the immersion phase of caregiving.

There will come a time when the person you care so deeply for may no longer be able to do even simple tasks for themselves, and you'll long for those times when they were still independent. Surprisingly, what might seem unobtainable for them may be possible with patience and a little bit of encouragement on your part. Instead of thinking you always need to assist, think about encouraging them to keep trying and then celebrate each time they accomplish one of these seemingly difficult, but do-able, tasks.

When Gwen had difficulty brushing her teeth in the later stages of her disease, we found a solution for her to complete this task by using an electric toothbrush and taking all the time she wanted. It became even more comfortable and convenient when I placed a stool in front of the bathroom sink. As effortless as these modifications may seem, it was gratifying to see the impact on her as she experienced a sense of accomplishment.

Remember to pray for patience each day. Ask God to help you do those little things that can make such a big difference. Remember 1 Corinthians 13:4: "Love is patient, love is kind." Ask God to help you; be understanding, make every attempt to be encouraging, and think about being supportive no matter what happens.

Most of all, focus your attention on doing everything through-out the day with a loving attitude. There will no doubt be times when your frustration level skyrockets, but stop and offer up a breath prayer as a way of calming yourself down. Ask God to help you listen, understand, think, speak, and be more loving. By keeping these things in mind, you'll find that patience comes more easily and can make each day a little less challenging and a little more rewarding for both of you.

Begin each day by giving it to God. In addition to asking for patience, ask Him to give you the strength, wisdom, energy, and guidance to be the caregiver you want to be. At the same time, continue developing your spiritual practices. Spend time in prayer with your loved one. Openly express your challenges and concerns while asking them to be just as open in voicing their frustrations, needs, and concerns. Recognize your limitations by clearly voicing the fact that God is the one in control and that he knows the best plans and ways for you. Don't lose sight of what Jeremiah 29:11 says: "'For I know the plans I have for you,' declares the Lord, 'plans to prosper you and not to harm you, plans to give you hope and a future.'" Hold on to this promise in your heart.

Next, add passion to your caregiving style. Without passion you can find yourself just going through the motions of caregiving. Sure, you'll get the job done, but just getting the job done can soon feel like it's becoming a burden. Your efforts could slowly become devoid of joy.

Passion encourages exploration and empowers you to go above and beyond doing the basics. More importantly, passion leads to enthusiasm and enthusiasm builds confidence in both of you. Enthusiasm is infectious! One of our friends marveled at how her daytime caregiver arrived each morning filled with enthusiasm. Entering the door with a smile, a whistle, a donut, or a smoothie in her hand always set a positive tone.

Passion points the way to possibilities. Imagine the possibilities of what you can do, taking into consideration the realistic constraints you and your friend or loved one face rather than imagined limitations. This is what Patrice was struggling with. We encouraged her to begin thinking about doing things she and Damian used to enjoy while considering new possibilities.

A friend of ours shared how she and her family overcame a perceived limitation. Her husband had been confined to a hospital bed in the back room of their home. Since he was too big for her to physically lift him into his wheelchair, he had not been out of his room for several weeks. One evening their son, who was visiting from out of town, offered to lift his father out of bed and roll him into the dining room table. Once there, he was able to enjoy being with the family as they gathered for an evening meal. This little adventure of leaving his bedroom and heading down the hall to join the family for some together time turned out to be a special evening for everyone.

In some ways, caregiving is no different than any other relationship. If you want your relationship to stay positive and enjoyable, you need to broaden your thinking by being proactive and forward looking. You can make it flourish.

Don't Get Stuck in a Rut!

Always guard against the boredom that can come from monotonous routines. Ask yourself, "Are we doing the same things over and over again? Are we stuck in a rut?" When all you have to look forward to is doing the same old things, day in and day out, it can become discouraging for both you and your loved one. Due to physical limitations, monotony can easily begin to set in within any caregiving relationship.

While routines can be calming, don't automatically rule out the potential for change. No matter your situation, it's a good idea to think about and try little things you can change while change is still possible. It may take some trial and error to discover how much change to normal routines will be acceptable, so be willing to experiment. However, be aware that individuals suffering from Alzheimer's disease and other forms of dementia may find change to be especially stressful in the final stages of their disease. In these types of situations, you may need to maintain a sense of predictability. If you begin noticing that changes are creating more stress than joy, you can always settle back into your comfortably predictable routines.

Start thinking now about little things you can do to add a bit of mystery and excitement to your everyday routines. Once again, this is another opportunity for your vitals to step in with helpful suggestions and encouragement to try something new. Seek their input for ideas on things to do that are feasible as well as those things that could be fun, inspiring, or even a little challenging.

When Catherine was helping to care for a shut-in friend, she felt her friend's restlessness and need for a change in routine. They discovered that taking a drive around town helped break up their routines and brightened up the day. Then, after driving by all of their favorite sights, they enjoyed stopping for lattes, adding a special treat to their outing.

Don't forget to celebrate each of these new adventures, no matter how small or insignificant you consider them to be. This is an opportunity for inclusion as you plan your days together. Take turns picking out a special event, outing, or project to do together. Always be open to those last-minute opportunities to do something different.

We can help you start thinking about new things to try, then you can experiment and add to our list. Some of our suggestions will work for both men and women, while others are probably more gender specific. Would any of the following easy-to-do ideas work for you and your loved one?

- Ask a friend to stop by for a fun visit
- Find a new game to play (cards, board game, or computer game)
- Pick up a bouquet of flowers from the store to surprise your loved one (or cut flowers from your garden, or order a delivery of flowers)
- Bring home a favorite food like dessert or a special coffee or tea to enjoy together
- Complete crossword puzzles together
- Put together a jigsaw puzzle
- Listen to music
- Watch TV together
- Something else (you fill in the blank)

You could also think about doing things together like painting nails. Yes, sons and husbands, I did this, and you can too. Looking at old scrapbooks, yearbooks, or sorting through old photos can lead to opportunities for storytelling and sharing. Memories can be triggered through seeing these pictures. This can also be an opportunity for creating new memory albums, digital photo albums, or digital postings.

As you engage in activities for enjoyment (or to redirect attention for loved ones with cognitive disorders), pay close attention to finding ones that aren't too difficult. This will take patience and experimentation on your part, but the rewards found in meaningful involvement and trying something new are worth the effort. Look for new things to do and change up your routine!

Venture Out!

Don't give up being socially active or going out in public as long as it's physically possible. This may be difficult if you need to make special accommodations or if either of you have a tendency to be introverted, but it's important for both of you. Venturing out often becomes even more difficult in the later immersion phase of caregiving. However, it may still be possible with planning and creativity. If you find it difficult to maneuver in crowds and need more time to get settled in at your destination, plan to arrive early. If you're going someplace new, try checking it out beforehand and planning ahead to avoid the unexpected. When you know that additional assistance will be needed, this is a good time to call on one of your vitals, constants, or reachables who might be attending the same event or activity.

If you're dealing with a walker or a wheelchair, accessibility to public buildings and facilities is always a concern. Luckily the provisions in government-mandated disabilities acts have made accessibility to most public places a possibility. However, this does not apply to historic structures. Even with these mandated changes, there could be some unique challenges when using public and private transportation. There could be stairs, escalators, gaps at platforms, busses that can't "kneel" to the curb, narrow aisles on airplanes, or any number of unforeseen obstacles.

Don't panic, plan ahead (check websites or call), and if things don't turn out as planned, politely ask for assistance. I always found workable solutions or alternatives by locating someone in charge or asking people if they were regular customers for ideas and alternatives. If you're traveling long distances or there's a change in personnel, always keep anyone new apprised of your needs. Surprises can be upsetting for everyone. Approaching a real or perceived obstacle with the idea of finding a solution takes away excuses for not venturing out.

The major reason we heard for not venturing out was dealing with the dreaded restroom break, especially when assistance was needed. Finding convenient, comfortable, and clean restrooms seems to be a common concern for both caregivers and their loved ones. While finding a solution to this dilemma may appear to be a difficult hurdle at first, you'll discover this is a challenge that can be easily overcome. You can almost always find accessible stalls in both men's and women's restrooms. If you need to accompany them, all you need to do is announce that your assistance is required and before entering say something like, "Man on board," or "Woman coming in to assist," and then pause for a response before stepping in.

For safety and/or cleanliness reasons, service stations or public restrooms may not be the best choices. Instead, consider visitor's centers, hotel lobbies, libraries, supermarkets, or truck stops as better alternatives. Yes, truck stops. We found truck stops to be especially accommodating when pushing a wheelchair. They have very clean and private shower/bathroom combinations and always seem willing to offer a key as a courtesy (at no charge) when asked.

We continue to be amazed at how helpful and understanding the general public is when they see you struggling or in need of help, or even if you simply explain what kind of help you need. Whenever a need was announced, neither Gwen nor I ever encountered a situation where we weren't offered assistance. Sometimes while searching for ways to overcome real or perceived obstacles, the creativity of strangers brought about unexpected joys of triumph! We have even had custodians and gate agents at airports and rail stations shut down an entire restroom and guard the door for our convenience. As we were leaving, they all had a similar parting statement, "Have a blessed day," and then they would let the waiting line file in.

Strengthened with the confidence to venture out, consider looking into and participating in some of the following activities, outings, and events that can easily change up your routine by:

- Going to a sporting event or concert
- Going on a sight-seeing tour
- Going on a picnic
- Going on a fishing trip
- Going to a movie
- Trying a new restaurant
- Exploring a museum
- Taking a walk or pushing a wheelchair around the block or in a park
- Going to the mall or store to just look around or even shop
- Going to the library or bookstore and browsing for new books or videos to watch

Be creative, tapping your imagination while selecting useful ideas that others might have offered. The possibilities are endless. Just like Patrice and Damian discovered, they created moments of joy.

Be bold in your thinking. Don't accept the status quo and don't let anyone tell you something can't be done. Being bold doesn't always mean doing things that are earth-shattering. It means just doing something that takes you away from your normal routine. Come up with ideas for unexpected, pleasant little things to surprise the person you are caring for.

We know from experience that almost any obstacle can be overcome. Finding solutions adds a sense of enjoyment and

achievement. Your perceived limits of what can be done and accomplished may not be limits at all; they could simply be restric-
tions you've created in your mind. With a little imagination and
ingenuity, almost anything is possible. The old admonition that
"we have met the enemy and the enemy is us" is especially true
when it comes to caregiving. So, consider the possibilities and
not the obstacles. I faced many a staircase while pushing a wheelchair and wondered if there was any way to get to the top. What
fun it was to see Gwen smile as perfect strangers suggested another route or offered to help me carry the wheelchair to the top
and back down again later.

The importance of considering possibilities and ignoring perceived limits became crystal clear when our friends accompanied us on a picnic/fishing trip. Their teenage daughter, who has
cerebral palsy, was watching her dad and me fish. She kept asking to try, but her dad said that there was no way she'd be able to
crank the reel if she caught one. I convinced him to let her try.
When she hooked that first fish, the squeals of delight and her
unforeseen ability to reel it in delighted all of our hearts! It was a
time of celebration. I smiled, and remembered that with God, all
things are possible (Matthew 19:26).

* * * * *

Pause for Prayer

Dear Lord, thank You for the opportunity to pause and pray. Fill me with the hope, peace, strength, courage, and boldness to be the caregiver I need to be. Help me to be patient, understanding, and encouraging in ways that make a meaningful difference and allow (my loved one) to be understood and loved. Help us to keep our focus on You and to look for creative ways to find contentment in our days. Thank You for being there to hear our prayers and concerns. Amen.

CHAPTER SEVEN

Be Creative and Encouraging

*It's not how much you do, but how much love you
put in the doing.*
Mother Teresa

W hat does the term "user-friendly" mean to you? We've all come to expect ramps, automatic doors, special seating, and designated parking spaces to meet the needs of people with disabilities. The importance of these adaptations and user-friendly facilities became obvious as Gwen became wheelchair dependent. When we encountered facilities that were truly user-friendly, it quickly became obvious that whoever designed them did more than what was legally required. They had been very deliberate in creating facilities that kept in mind the comfort, dignity, and needs of users with disabilities and physical limitations.

You'll know what I mean if you've ever pushed a wheelchair into a restroom stall marked handicapped. It can be disappointing to discover that the only difference between that stall and a regular stall is that it's a few inches wider and has a grab bar on the back wall. Compare this to an accessible stall that has room for the wheelchair and a companion along with multiple grab bars. You'll quickly appreciate the planning and thoughtfulness that has gone into meeting special needs.

The same attention to user-friendly details becomes immediately apparent when entering accessible hotel rooms. I've noticed there are two types of accessible rooms. There are rooms that meet only the legal accessibility regulations, and there are other rooms that are truly user-friendly and provide other thoughtful touches. These rooms comply with the Americans with Disabilities Act, having peep holes placed in lower levels in the doors so someone in a wheelchair can see out. They also have lights that flash so the hearing impaired will know when someone is "knocking" on the door. They have a raised toilet with grab bars, as well as grab bars in the tub/shower area. If the room wasn't built with a roll-in shower, you can ask for, and usually get, a shower chair.

You'll also notice many other significant differences and thoughtful attention to details:

- Instead of a bed that is a foot off the floor, it is flush with the floor for ease of getting in and out.
- In addition to having grab bars available in the bathroom, someone has actually thought about where these grab bars should be placed so they are functional.
- Instead of locating the handicapped room at the end of a hallway, it is located next to the elevator or only a few steps from the lobby.

All of this user-friendly attention to detail in public and private spaces makes a big difference. Have you thought about the importance of these same types of considerations in your home? How can you provide for your loved one's physical and emotional needs? Are there things you should change? You can start answering these questions by looking at your physical living space from your loved one's perspective.

Create a User-Friendly Living Space

If you were asked to describe your comfy, no hassle, feel good place, you could probably list several descriptive adjectives. Would this be the same list for your loved one? Why not ask them? When you have their input and begin thinking about these descriptions, what actions can you take to make them possible?

Begin by considering how to provide the same level of attention professionals do in creating user-friendly spaces focused on the real needs of users like your loved one. You can do the same thing and make a big difference in your loved one's comfort by paying the same level of attention to these details. So, when it comes to making your living space user-friendly, where should you start?

Look at your living spaces through your loved one's eyes. Think about everything you can see and touch from their point of view. Ask yourself some basic questions. How many steps are there to negotiate before you get to the front door? Is there a ramp and are there handrails? Are the doors and hallways wide enough to accommodate a wheelchair? Are there physical barriers that block ease of movement in commonly used living spaces? Are there grab bars in the bathroom? Do you have a bathtub or shower with easy access? Do you have a bathtub bench or a shower chair?

Now, think about other things that can make life easier and safer. For example, do you have nightlights in hallways and bathrooms? Is lighting bright, cheery, and inviting? Do you need to install higher wattage bulbs, or more light fixtures or lamps? Do you have a bed rail? Would a hospital bed make your lives easier? Do you have sturdy handrails in all stairways? Could a chair lift be installed if you need to use multiple floors? Have you thought about getting a swivel seat to ease the problems of getting into and out of a chair or vehicle? Would a reclining lift chair make getting up and down out of a chair easier?

I knew about the need to make many of these potential modifications but waited far too long to make one in particular that ended up having a significant positive impact on Gwen. It involved the conversion of a bathtub to a roll-in shower. For someone who is able-bodied, the fourteen- to sixteen-inch step up into a bathtub may seem like no big deal. For someone with aging or mobility issues, making that same step up can seem like trying to climb Mount Everest. When I finally made this modification, it made our lives so much easier.

If you are caring for someone who is dealing with advanced Alzheimer's disease or other forms of dementia, consider making some helpful modifications. Think about installing door locks (it may require more than one), acquiring a patient monitor, decluttering, and removing visual cues that could prompt wandering behaviors. Place keys, coats, wallets/purses, shoes, and other similar items that might bring up thoughts of leaving home out of sight. Remove mirrors, items that cast shadows, and other visual stimuli that could create distractions. All of these modifications can reduce impulses to step outside, become confused, and stray away.

By paying attention to your loved one's needs and behaviors, you can discover other user-friendly modifications to address living space challenges. The point is, always be looking at your living space and searching for creative ideas to make it more accommodating and inviting. While searching, don't forget the importance that cleanliness, cheerful colors, flowers, and natural lighting can have on enhancing a person's mood.

In addition to addressing the comfort and functionality of your loved one's surroundings, also be thinking about other actions to improve your overall caregiving environment. Our friend Piper frequently talked about the mood-enhancing benefits of aromatherapy. She always made sure we had an assortment of scented candles, oils, and hand and body lotions. When she visited Gwen, she would apply these lotions to her hands and arms. The conversations, physical contact, and presence of these soothing scents always helped stimulate feelings of connection and comfort for Gwen. Visitors often commented on the way this also made the house feel so inviting and peaceful.

Find Time for Fun

Relax, rejoice, let go, laugh, smile, and find time for fun. The blessings that flow from having fun and participating in engaging activities are sure to bring moments of joy and a smile. Have you thought about tapping the benefits of music, dance, and other artistic activities to create an encouraging caregiving atmosphere?

It's been said that music is medicine for the soul. The power of music to heal and comfort is truly a gift from God. Music can have a deep personal impact, transforming hearts and souls by slowing your heart rate, lowering your blood pressure, and helping your body relax. It can even soothe away your worries and provide a positive boost to your mood. It also has the power to reduce stress, depression, tension, fatigue, anger, and confusion.

Listening to and singing along together with your loved one is another opportunity for promoting communication and harmony. Sometimes it's fun to just hum the melody of a song if the words are forgotten or too difficult to form. Singing is also a very effective voice exercise for strengthening vocal cords and enhancing clarity of speech. Don't underestimate the power of music to make a meaningful difference. Music gives joy and encouragement throughout the day!

Music can also be effective in improving memory and cognition. This became very apparent while sitting in church one Sunday. Gwen and I often sat behind an older woman who was showing signs of Alzheimer's disease. She usually sat quietly with her daughter, head down, and seemed to be unresponsive most of the time. But one week she caught my attention when we began singing "How Great Thou Art." She perked up and sang all the verses without looking at a single word. Her face was full of joy and happiness as she truly was worshiping God with all her heart.

I was amazed at how she did this; even I had to follow the words on the screen. It was obvious I didn't have them memorized. When we left the service, I wondered if the woman's daughter had noticed the same thing I had and was playing her mom's favorite hymns at home on a regular basis. It's a known fact that a person with Alzheimer's disease can hear a song that somehow triggers their memories, prompting them to sing along.

Ask anyone to tell you the names of their favorite songs, artists, or styles of music, and you never have to worry about getting a response. Even if you think you know the songs and types of music the person you are caring for enjoys, ask them to name their favorites. Based on their response, you can create a collection of songs and make playlists for their tablet, phone, or computer to listen to anywhere and anytime.

It's amazing to see how much joy music brings to the listener. This joy becomes even more evident when listening to the words and melodies of inspirational and worship music. These familiar tunes will calm hearts, giving a sense of peace. They allow a person to feel and experience God's presence and healing touch. They're reminders of God's presence, love, promises, and faithfulness.

In addition to listening to or playing music, what other types of fun creative activities would be interesting to your loved one? Could they benefit from creating an artistic piece, actively participating in dancing, or seeing others dance? Which of these activities would bring them joy and put a smile on their face? Can they do these activities on their own or would they find it easier to participate in professionally organized and managed therapy programs?

Just like music, art and dance can be enjoyed individually or with each other. Creating artistic pieces is not only fun, but it can also improve hand dexterity, mood, and quality of life by opening up opportunities to communicate thoughts and feelings. In addition, artistic creations provide peaceful and calming thoughts, often serving as a stimulus to recall happy memories. Dance has the power to actively engage participants in movement as well as helping with balance and coordination. The physical closeness and joy experienced in dancing creates feelings of connectivity and living in the moment. Even silly dancing in the kitchen or living room can bring a smile to everyone's face.

Gwen enjoyed creating counted cross stitch and needlepoint works of art, but there was no question that live music and choreographed performances brought her the greatest joy. Even before she was wheelchair bound, I purchased season tickets to a nearby community theater. There were some performances that I was not particularly drawn to, but watching the joy she experienced each time we attended any of these performances was well worth my time and effort.

One caregiver described how much joy painting brought to her husband. Even when he could no longer hold a paint brush, the two of them had wonderful afternoons creating art by finger painting. She smiled when describing how these carefree moments, filled with laughter and fun, created feelings of encouragement and hope.

Another caregiver we knew always talked about how dancing had been an important part of his wife's life. They danced when they could, but when she couldn't dance anymore, they took time together to watch musicals and especially the TV show *Dancing with the Stars*. Even though his loved one was wheelchair bound, she would still join in the excitement by watching others and tapping her feet with delight and joy.

With a little bit of experimentation, you'll find what brings the most joy to your loved one. Some activities you might consider include painting, drawing, cross stitch, crocheting, jewelry-making, coloring, chalkboard art, flower arranging, Play-Doh/clay molding, scrapbooking, watching shows about cake decorating,

old sock hop dances, ballet, photography, cooking, or home reno-
vation projects.

Whether these activities are self-directed or facilitated
through professionally staffed programs, they provide additional
opportunities for you and your loved one to:

- Relax and experience a sense of calmness and well-being
- Take your mind off of the difficulties of the day
- Reduce levels of anxiety and depression
- Sometimes reduce aches and physical pains
- Change the focus and pace of the day

Don't underestimate the positive power that creative activities can have in making your loved one's care journey more enjoyable. Remember, anything you can do to encourage partici-
patory activities is therapeutic and provides opportunities for
accomplishment and another way of connecting with the person
you are caring for.

Include Prayer

We've encouraged you to pray and asked you to "pause for
prayer" at the end of each chapter. As we discussed in Chapter
Four, prayer is the most important thing you can do as a caregiver to begin your day, take with you throughout your day, and
end your day. Prayer is just as important for you as it is for your
loved one.

Philippians 4:6 says, "Do not be anxious about anything, but
in everything, by prayer and petition, with thanksgiving, present
your requests to God." Gwen and I found that starting the day in
prayer together drew us closer to each other. Praying also helped
us feel closer and more connected to God throughout the day.

God is faithful to hear your prayers; no concern is too trivial
for Him. Lift up your needs as well as those of your loved one
to Him. Praying and being in God's presence brings a calming

stillness to your lives, creating a quiet center of peace within both of you. As you move back into the busyness of the day, take this peaceful centeredness with you. Knowing that you have God's sense of presence with you empowers you and strengthens you.

Consider using the method of "praying Scripture" as a straightforward and comfortable way of praying with or for your loved one. Inserting your loved one's name in a Scripture passage and praying it out loud opens you to God's presence in a deeper way. It acknowledges God's guidance, love, peace, comfort, and hope for you and your loved one in a very personal sense.

Psalm 23 is a good example of a Bible passage that can be used for praying Scripture. As you read this psalm, substitute the name of the person you are praying for (or even your name) for the pronouns *me*, *I*, *my*, and *you*. Give it a try. Begin by reaching out to hold their hand or touch their shoulder. Then slowly read this passage out loud using their name in place of the pronouns.

Psalm 23:1–6

The Lord is _____'s shepherd; _____ shall not be in want.
The Lord makes _____ lie down in green pastures,
He leads _____ beside quiet waters,
He restores _____ soul. He guides _____ in paths of righteousness for his name's sake.
Even though _____ walks through the valley of the shadow of death, _____ will fear no evil, for you are with _____;
Your rod and your staff, they comfort _____.
You prepare a table before _____ in the presence of _____ enemies.
You anoint _____ head with oil; _____'s cup overflows.
Surely goodness and love will follow _____ all the days of _____'s life, and _____ will dwell in the house of the Lord forever.

There are several other Bible passages that work well for praying Scripture. Try selecting one or all of the following passages and practice until it becomes a natural and comfortable way of praying:

- Psalm 139:13–18
- Ephesians 3:16–20
- Psalm 121:1–8
- Isaiah 43:1–3a

Encourage your vitals, constants, and even visitors to read the Bible and pray this way with your loved one. When God nudged us to do this, we noticed what a powerful impact it had on the person being prayed for—and on anyone else who was present in the room. Anytime I saw Gwen being prayed for in this way, I could see the comfort it brought her. A sense of peace always settled over her. These feelings of comfort and peace never got old. Hearing her name read in Scripture affected her so deeply. Anyone who was present at the time was touched in much the same way, even to the point of shedding tears. It always seemed to create a sense of calmness, providing openings for meaningful connections, discussions, and further prayer.

We also found this to be an opportunity to allow those who find it difficult to pray in the presence of others to feel more at ease while praying. When praying using Scripture, the pressure of having to know what to say or how to say it is removed. This is a meaningful way for others to pray God's Word over your loved one. It can also comfort someone whom you seek to reassure and encourage.

Just Be There

The most meaningful gift any of us can give someone who is suffering and in need of care is our presence. It's a way of showing a person they are loved and that they matter. It's a way of saying,

"I'm here. I may not have the answers or be able to provide a fix for the difficulties you face, but I'm here." As the keystone caregiver, if you are intentional, you are already there with your loved one on a deep and meaningful level.

If you're not the keystone caregiver and are just stepping in to help, remember the importance your presence makes. As we saw with Piper's caring touches, just the act of being there was so powerful and meaningful to Gwen. The nice thing about being there is that it doesn't take any special training or skills on your part. Simply reaching out and touching your loved one's arm or hand and looking into their eyes lets them know you are there and that you love and care about them. A challenge you may face is learning when and how to be there without being intrusive. You can learn this by being observant and noticing when they become tired or when it becomes difficult for them to engage.

What God allows to happen in situations when you show up and care for someone is a wonderful experience for everyone. Kara Tippets and Jill Lynn Buteyn say this throughout their book, *Just Show Up: The Dance of Walking Through Suffering Together*. The impact you can have on another person's life will bless both of you far beyond anything you've ever imagined.

When Catherine asked God to show her how she could connect with her two friends that had Parkinson's disease, she felt Him nudging her in small ways. First, there was a nudge to bring them a meal. Then there were nudges to take flowers, to send a note, or just to stop by for a visit. She felt God saying to her, "Just show up. I am with you and will help you express that you care. Let me minister through you."

Even though she was not the keystone caregiver in these situations, she often found that these caring visits turned into a deeper involvement, resulting in sweet, never-to-be-forgotten journeys of walking with her friends in their times of suffering. Sometimes they would just sit together in silence. At other times they shared favorite Bible verses and prayed together. No matter how they spent their time together, it led to deeper spiritual friendships.

Although she was timid at first, Catherine would have missed out on these sacred bonding times had she not listened to God's nudges to just show up. The same was true for me. Family members of so many loved ones we have spent time with have since reflected on the significance of these visits and how much our presence and "just being there" meant to them as well. They were comforted and felt the blessing of being cared for, too.

As the keystone caregiver, you may need to remind yourself of how important your focused attention is to your loved one. For your part, turn off the TV, lay the magazine aside, and put down your mobile device. Then, without any distractions, just be there for your loved one for a few quiet moments. Do this multiple times throughout the day. Remember, your calming and comforting presence will be a powerful and meaningful gift both physically and emotionally.

Pay Attention

Pay attention to how your loved one responds to everyone and everything that is happening around them. Watch closely to see how they respond to people and how they enjoy or don't enjoy their company. Don't assume they only enjoy certain people. Ask them how and why they enjoy or don't enjoy being around and interacting with different people.

Listen closely to everything they say as well as what they don't say. Look for clues to gain a better understanding of their preferences by learning their body language and paying close attention to the look in their eyes. Developing these observational skills becomes even more important in the immersion and release phases of caregiving as verbal skills can often diminish. Don't forget, as the keystone caregiver, team captain, and gatekeeper, you have at least some control over who and what types of interactions occur with your loved one.

As we've mentioned, body language and the eyes can speak volumes without ever saying a word. People would always say they could see the joy Gwen was experiencing by simply looking at her smile and the twinkle in her eyes. Those same eyes could also easily convey anxiety, frustration, disgust, or discomfort. Then there were the frowns or the sighs that would definitely get my attention and alert me with an unspoken plea to take care of a need or concern I hadn't noticed. However, the most important thing I could see when looking at her was that she loved me and was content, knowing I was there to care for her.

Recognizing and knowing the meaning of changes in body language also lets you know if your loved one is enjoying being with people or is tiring of an experience, an event, or an outing. You'll soon learn when it's time to end a visit, the outing, or the task at hand. You can intervene by redirecting the activity or graciously ending a conversation or visit.

I soon learned to know when Gwen was tired and ready to go home or didn't want to continue a task or extend a conversation. She didn't have to say anything. I could tell what she wanted by looking at her. Developing this level of understanding made it easier for me to know when she was having a good or a bad experience.

You'll know better than anyone else when your loved one is tired and needs space. You can provide this needed space by controlling the stream of people, calls, messages, etc. at a level that doesn't drain your loved one's energy. Begin monitoring their needs and desires, regulating the busyness that swirls around the realities of caregiving. That way when your loved one says "No" and "I've had enough," you'll know that they really mean "No" and "I've had enough."

Stay Positive

Finally, enhance your caring environment with a liberal dose of positivity! Being intentional means never giving up, even when things seem overwhelming. Saying you will stay positive is one of those things that is easy to say but at times difficult to do. The downside of any difficult caregiving challenge will always be there, but you can remain positive by making a conscious effort not to dwell on the negatives. Remaining positive by always looking for something that is at least a little bit encouraging in every situation makes everyday challenges seem a little easier.

Failing to focus on the positives can easily lead to a self-defeating cycle of arguing, blaming, and complaining. Don't fall into this self-defeating, "woe is me" trap. There'll always be negative things that can easily creep into your thoughts and weigh on your mind as you progress through your caregiving journey. Don't waste your energy rehashing negative events or hurtful comments. Instead, focus your energies and attention on the positives. Stay lighthearted, finding opportunities to add a touch of humor to everyday activities. Laughter, playfulness, and moments of spontaneous joy can ease even the most difficult situations.

This can be difficult, as there will be days filled with discomfort and pain. There will also be those hard days when one or both of you will feel sad, tired, or hopeless. So, how do you go about avoiding these negative traps and staying positive? As simple as it sounds, a small mental or physical break could make a big difference in the way you feel. This could be one of those times when you need to reach out and ask someone to step in, giving you that precious time to regroup and refresh yourself.

Another way of staying positive is to remember that God is in your lives. Spend time reading the promises of God in the Bible. Underline or highlight them if it helps. He promises that we need not be dismayed or afraid (Isaiah 41:10). He promises to always be with us (Joshua 1:5). He promises to give us strength (Isaiah 40:29). He promises that His peace will guard our hearts and minds (Philippians 4:7). God's promises never fail to meet our needs.

We also found it important and refreshing to constantly be looking for blessings in our lives, no matter how small they may be, and we hope you'll do this too. Seeing a rainbow or other reminders of God's presence and love (butterflies, the color yellow, certain birds, chimes, etc.) always made us smile and encouraged us. Sharing devotionals, listening to Christian radio, and watching uplifting TV programs and movies with those we cared for always helped us to think positively.

Remember to keep yourself grounded and growing in your faith by beginning and ending each day together with a prayer of thanksgiving. One of the ways we found to end each day on a positive note was to ask, "What is one thing that happened today for which you/we are thankful?" If an answer doesn't immediately come to mind, don't skip this opportunity to be thankful for an uneventful day. If you take a little quiet time to be reflective, you may find that an answer will eventually come to one of you. It could be a day without pain, a day without nausea, or a quiet day of rest.

As the symptoms of Gwen's Parkinson's disease progressed, we had many opportunities to become negative. There was no denying that we were faced with new and increasingly demanding challenges. These challenges became more obvious as we moved through the reliance and into the immersion phase. However, rather than dwelling on what was no longer possible, we focused our attention on changes we could make to cope with the difficulties we faced.

For example, through the years we moved from a walking stick (we never called it a cane), to a walker, to a wheelchair for longer distances, and then finally to a wheelchair full-time. Even though each of these progressive changes could have been demoralizing, we both stayed positive and focused on the blessings of mobility and more. When close friends and even casual acquaintances asked, "How do you stay so positive," our answer was always the same.

"Our faith."

Sure, we always hoped and prayed for a cure, and we encourage you to hold on to your hopes as you pray for a cure. But in many cases, such as ours, hope for a cure will be just that, a hope that at best will be for someone else in the distant future. As difficult as it may seem, coming to grips with the fact that many conditions and diseases are progressively degenerative is a major step toward acceptance. This opens the way for nurturing an effective, faith-based, intentional caregiving partnership.

Catherine's mother, who was elderly and dealing with age-related difficulties, liked to say to Catherine, "We're in this together. I'm so glad I have you." Gwen also said virtually the same thing to me on many different occasions during the immersion and release phases of our journey. My response would always be, "I love you and look forward to every new day and the adventures that await us."

If anyone knew when they started their caregiving journey what the entire scope of caregiving might look like from beginning to end, many, if not most, would give up before ever beginning. However, as Catherine and I look back, we can both say we would willingly do it all over again. We found encouragement many times from remembering God's promises and the words of Psalm 54:4: "God is the one who sustains me."

* * * * *

Pause for Prayer

Dear Lord, thank You that You sustain us and continue to be with us in this journey. Help us not to be anxious about anything but instead come to You in prayer about everything. Help us to remember the importance of laughing, smiling, and finding time for fun. Help us stay positive and find ways to encourage each other. Thank You for the blessings You give us and for the daily reminders of Your presence and love. Amen.

CHAPTER EIGHT

Reach Out for Extra Help

There are only four kinds of people in the world.
Those who have been caregivers. Those who are
currently caregivers. Those who will be caregivers,
and those who will need a caregiver.
Roslyn Carter

As a caregiver, have you ever felt lonely or isolated? Even with a great care team and a loving circle of supporters, it can happen. Have you ever thought, "Nobody understands what we go through every day, not even family and friends." Are there days when you get up thinking, "I know I can do it, but it sure would be nice if I could find a way to take a break." These aren't unique thoughts. These are commonly expressed caregiver feelings.

As Catherine spent more time with Gwen and me and with other caregivers and their loved ones, she began hearing and sensing these frustrations and concerns. Then, while reading stories about the life and ministry of Mother Teresa, she was inspired by how this deeply compassionate person was able to impact the lives of so many lonely and isolated people. Mental images from these stories served as God's reminders for Catherine to be on the lookout for those in need of encouragement and connections. From then on, she made it a point to reach out to people who mentioned they needed help, lacked supportive connections, were unintentionally overlooked, or were in need of encouragement.

When her own mother was homebound and became isolated, Catherine witnessed what a difference it made in her mother's life when people stopped by to help or check in on her. She saw how the supportive connections from these people who reached out were a great source of encouragement and demonstration of love for her mother.

Both you and your loved one can avoid isolation and continue to flourish by maintaining connections that flow from interactions. Think about remaining active and engaged by intentionally reaching out to and being with others. Things like going to church and Bible studies, attending support groups, meeting a friend for coffee or lunch, or visiting with extended family can build and strengthen relationships. We found that these activities opened up opportunities for others to be supportive and to offer their help with daily caregiving.

Those of you who are comfortable reaching out for help will easily find people who are ready to engage with you and your loved one. For others, reaching out may be more of a challenge. It may feel uncomfortable, as the effort required can be time-consuming and intimidating. It may take a special effort on your part to step out of your comfort zone, reach out, and welcome others in. Like Catherine's mother experienced, the benefits can be inspiring, comforting, and life-changing.

It All Adds Up!

Stepping into the role of caregiver probably found you doing many things out of necessity or just to be helpful. Eventually, simply helping out turned into more demanding requirements as your loved one progressively looked to you for more assistance. Taking on more and more can lead you toward what seems to be

an overwhelming mountain of challenges. You may find yourself being caught up in what feels like a juggling act while you
struggle to coordinate multiple demands on your time. You know
you want to do your best and don't want to drop any of the balls,
however there are realistic limits to your time and energy.

This sharpened focus on caregiving can easily lead to feelings
of isolation and loneliness. There's also the risk of feeling un-
appreciated or even being taken for granted—not only by your
loved one, but also by those who are unaware of all you do. At
some point it may seem like there aren't enough hours in the day
to get everything accomplished. When the daily challenges of
caregiving are stacked on top of everyday demands (especially
when these tasks span many years), they can eventually result in
a downpour of negative emotions. These emotions can range all
the way from anger, anxiety, irritability, and sadness to feelings
of hurt, resentment, despair, and grief.

These feelings can be especially heightened when a loved one
doesn't appear to recognize or acknowledge that you're trying to
help. When the everyday demands of caregiving begin weighing you down, remember the words of Deuteronomy 31:8: "The
Lord himself goes before you and will be with you . . . Do not be
afraid; do not be discouraged." Lift up your concerns through
prayer and turn them over to God.

When negative feelings begin to surface, take time to acknowledge and process them. It may help to write them down or share
them with one of your vitals. Expressing these feelings and having them validated is important in helping to maintain your self-
worth as well as your physical and emotional energy. Although
your efforts may not be affirmed, be encouraged knowing that
you're providing invaluable services and support.

Both Catherine and I have seen too many situations where
keystone caregivers found themselves overwhelmed with daily
challenges and failed to reach out and ask for help. The outcome
can be similar to what happened to the frog in the following

story. As you read this story, think about your current situation and see if it applies to you.

> *Once there was a frog who was snatched from his pond and placed in a sack. From the sack, he was put into a large pot of water. At first, he was happy. He was out of the sack. The water felt good. He was comfortable. Little did he know that a fire had been lit under his comfortable pot.*
>
> *Gradually, ever so gradually, the water temperature was constantly rising. First it was just a little bit warmer, not much different than a soft, sunny, late spring day. Then the water got much warmer, like a breezeless, sunbaked August afternoon.*
>
> *He began to feel a little uncomfortable, but the changes were happening so slowly he didn't even notice. As his discomfort grew, he could have jumped out of the pot, but he didn't. The water finally got so hot he couldn't jump. Before he knew it, he was cooked!*

Have you ever found yourself feeling like this frog? Are things changing around you that you aren't noticing? If you aren't careful, you too could face a similar fate to that of the frog. You could become so engrossed in caregiving duties that you start feeling overwhelmed, eventually becoming resentful or discouraged.

Kelly and Patrice were both heading down this path. However, they saw what was happening and accepted help. Do you remember how beneficial those extra helping hands were for them? That same type of help can be there for you. When you start feeling overwhelmed, remember to reach out to your care team and ask for help. Lean on your vitals for physical and emotional support. In addition, voice your frustrations and concerns to God. He is always there to help share your load.

Embrace Suggestions

From our experiences and discussions with other caregivers, we found that observations and suggestions from people who see you on a regular basis can be surprisingly helpful. They can see and observe with fresh eyes things that are said and unsaid as well as some body language you might miss. Don't be shy. It's okay to encourage and even ask them to help you notice things you might be overlooking. Ask them to come along beside you and honestly tell you what they see.

Being open to and listening to others made life easier for Gwen. She loved to read. When turning pages became difficult, we switched from physical books to ordering books on her Kindle. Then, a close friend suggested getting audio books from the library. I took his advice. This provided new opportunities for her to continue enjoying one of her favorite activities. This same friend also provided other useful ideas when he noticed us struggling with awkward or challenging situations. One of these suggestions included getting a swiveling seat pad, making it easier to get in and out of the car.

Listen closely to helpful advice given by your vitals. However, be prepared to receive a lot of suggestions from other well-meaning people as well. Avoid being dismissive when they say things you may not be ready to hear or have already heard too many times. With your focus on caregiving, it's very easy to inadvertently hurt their feelings by giving a quick negative response or no response at all to their suggestions and offers of help.

They may think they're being helpful, but because of their lack of understanding of the circumstances you and your loved one face, their suggestions may seem like nothing more than noise. Recognize that they may see things you've missed. Even if you know that some of their suggestions may seem to be totally inappropriate or undoable, it doesn't hurt to listen and think about them. Remember though, you're in charge and responsible for making any final decisions. You're still the gatekeeper!

When I was dealing with the day-to-day requirements of caregiving, I often heard comments like, "You should do it this way," or "Have you ever tried . . .?" While it was sometimes frustrating to hear these comments, I always tried to smile and thank those making them for their ideas. There were, however, times, especially after a long day or trying week, when their comments were a bit more than I could handle. There was even an occasional temptation to react negatively, but I tried not to.

Remind yourself that they care and really mean well. Remain gracious and ask yourself, "Have I become insensitive, or am I too set in my caregiving ways? Have I really considered trying what they're suggesting?" Don't intentionally discourage people who are trying to make helpful suggestions. Consider the possibility that there might be useful nuggets of wisdom in their ideas.

With the help of others, you can be clued into the need for changes that could easily be missed in your busyness. Don't be like the frog in the slowly warming pot; observe, listen, embrace suggestions, and be aware of the need for change. Proverbs 1:5 says, "Let the wise listen and add to their learning, and let the discerning get guidance." Proverbs 19:20 says, "Listen to advice and accept instruction, and in the end, you'll be counted among the wise." These verses caution us to listen to advice and add to our learning by accepting instruction.

Find Another You

The next time you start thinking you're the only one who can take care of your loved one, think about an experiment my mother challenged me to try when she saw me wearing myself out at work.

She said to begin by finding a good-sized bucket. Fill it with water, then let it sit for a minute or two before looking at it. The surface of the water should now be flat. Stick your hand into the water and shake it all around. The more you shake your hand, the bigger the ripples and the splashes get. Finally, take your hand out of the water and notice what happens. You'll notice that it doesn't take long for the surface of the water to once again become flat.

"Okay," you might say, "this is a cute experiment and a little bit messy, but what does it have to do with me and caregiving?" When you're an intentional caregiver, the tasks may become so all-consuming that you begin to think you're the only one who can take care of your loved one. You may even begin believing you're so important that if you aren't there to take care of everything, things just won't get done—or at least, won't get done the right way.

You could wear yourself out by constantly hovering and doing everything yourself, but sooner or later, whether you're shaking your hand in that bucket of water or caregiving for a loved one, you'll have to take a break. The alternative is finding yourself having to quit all together. Continuing to be in a state of constant motion will leave you exhausted and could eventually lead to resentment, or worse yet, burnout!

Before this exhaustion or burnout happens, consider reaching out to family, friends, or members of your church community for extra help. Look into the possibility of having them come by once or twice a week to visit. This could turn into weekly blocks of helping time or opportunities to assist with those little things that can be easier with an extra pair of hands. We have seen many church organizations, friends, and support groups organize and coordinate these visits and extra help through phone calls, volunteer sign-up sheets, and social media platforms.

At first I hesitated to ask friends to spend time with Gwen. However, I soon discovered that they always said yes when I did. They helped in so many different ways. They filled in for me, spending quality time with Gwen or taking her out to lunch, museums, movies, or girls' days out. It was apparent they wanted to give me a break by being with Gwen and involving her in their activities. I did my part by always trying to work around their schedules and never knowingly took advantage of their generosity.

Their time and thoughtful gestures made a huge difference in our days. These visits and breaks gave me time to socialize, run errands, or just have the freedom to take care of things on my to-do list. Don't forget that you need these breaks, and believe it or not, your loved one probably needs a break from you once in a while as well. Think about the benefits you'll experience when you come back together again, refreshed.

You can also explore finding someone who is qualified to come on a regularly scheduled basis, or as needed, to step in and fill your caregiving shoes. How and when you schedule this person(s) will depend on how often you need a break and the level of care needed by your loved one. For some, this will be a fairly easy task. For others, it will prove to be more difficult and require a great deal of planning and preparation. So, start planning now to find someone who can meet your loved one's needs and fit into your schedule.

In your search for fill-ins, you may be lucky enough to find the perfect match on your first try. Maybe it will be a family member, relative, friend, a private caregiver/companion, or someone from a caregiving service. If you find the perfect match on your first try, great! If you don't, be patient. Consider trying out a few people until you find the right one, or the right combination of people, to fill this important role in your caregiving team. Keep in mind that you are searching for someone who could eventually be considered a companion: someone who can monitor your loved one's needs and keep them company while you're away.

Just because someone cares about or has cared for a person with Alzheimer's disease, for example, doesn't mean they will be qualified or comfortable with caring for someone with Parkinson's disease. I can remember one fill-in caregiver who was professionally qualified, but her rough and abrupt actions made it seem like she didn't truly care. We tried her once and that was enough!

When trying out a fill-in caregiver for the first time, start out slow by taking just a couple of hours away. Be sure to leave detailed written instructions about what should be done and when, along with where you plan to be and your cell phone number. It's also a good idea to leave the cell phone number of one of your vitals, too. Don't plan to be very far away during this initial session so you can easily return on short notice if needed. You may want to stop back by after an hour or so just to check in. You can easily do this by going grocery shopping and then coming back to put things away. Even if you feel comfortable after a few sessions, it isn't a bad idea to also consider asking one of your confidants to stop by for a surprise visit just to see how things are going.

When you return, ask the person filling in for their impressions of how things went. Don't settle for platitudes like, "Okay," or "We had a good time together." Ask for specific examples of what went well or what seemed to be difficult or awkward. Then, after they leave, ask your loved one the same types of questions to find out how comfortable they felt with someone else taking care of them. Finally, ask yourself two questions: "Am I confident this person can take care of my loved one's specific condition and needs?" and "Would I feel comfortable leaving my loved one alone with this person all day?" When you can confidently say yes to these two questions, you'll gain the peace of mind needed to temporarily relinquish some of your duties.

There are some very important legal and financial issues that need to be considered when hiring a fill-in caregiver. This is especially important if you'll be paying this person more than $600 per year. For example, does your insurance provide coverage for a caregiver in your home? Will you need to withhold and/or make payments for social security, taxes, etc.? If these types of questions are concerning, consider hiring through an agency that can handle these issues for you.

Both Catherine and I have had multiple opportunities over the years to deal with many fill-in caregivers and we have witnessed the blessings the right ones can bestow on both caregivers and loved ones. This was especially true for me as almost everyone I selected to be with Gwen was strong in their faith. They knew God was a part of our lives, so they were willing to enthusiastically share their own inspirational stories of how God was a part of their lives, too!

Another important resource to consider when you need a break from your caregiving responsibilities is respite care. This is the ultimate opportunity to experience worry-free time for a few days, knowing all of your loved one's needs will be met. Respite care professionals are trained, licensed, and insured. Their services can be provided either in your home or in professional care facilities for either shorter or longer periods of time. It can be a time to catch up on sleep, evaluate your situation, think through your options, or to simply take time sitting with God. Time with God will renew you and fill you with a sense of peace. Remember His promise to always be with you, care for you, and to guide you. Isaiah 40:31 reminds us that "those who hope in the Lord will renew their strength."

Initiate Inclusion

The benefits of reaching out for extra help can be seen as people offer words of encouragement, show small acts of kindness, and treat your friend or loved one with dignity. This provides the extra touch of love and support that both of you need. The question is, how do you reach out and initiate these supportive connections that include others? How can you encourage people to feel comfortable in joining you in engaging with your loved one? Then, once engaged, how can you encourage them to stay involved?

Keep in mind that you will most likely be the one helping friends and visitors to become involved and engaged. For example, role modeling by asking them easy to answer questions is a good starting point for showing them how to initiate conversations. If you're stepping in to help the keystone caregiver, the same approach will work as well. This conversational style provides opportunities for getting to know each other and connecting on a more personal level. Here are some examples of questions that can lead to engaging conversations:

- Where were you born?
- Where did you grow up?
- What was your childhood like?
- What school(s) did you attend?
- What is your favorite song?
- What is your favorite color?
- What is your favorite Bible verse?

The resulting conversations create a springboard for hearing some interesting and often inspiring stories. In addition, questions about family (siblings, parents), favorite foods, movies, music, TV shows, books, and other things they like to do will open up possibilities for fun topics to talk about. Then, as they respond, pause to listen, maintain eye contact, nod, or ask additional questions that invite further conversation and clarification.

Friendships are formed and relationships are deepened as you and your loved one feel the love that flows around you. Thoughtful acts of kindness can often come from these interactions—even when you don't know they're needed!

Gwen and I experienced many unexpected gestures of kindness that came our way through these friendships. Things like a friend bringing by a hand-carved cross from his woodworking shop were especially meaningful. He even ended the visit with a prayer before he left. Visits like this were much-needed breaths of fresh air and welcomed breaks from our normal daily routines. We also found it comforting when people called, sent encouraging notes, emails, texts, or cards, reminding us they were thinking of us and praying for us. We told them on many occasions that these caring touches were often just as beneficial as a visit and were always loved and appreciated.

Catherine and I both know from personal experience how helpful and uplifting it is to have others share a cheerful word and a thoughtful prayer. Proverbs 16:24 reminds us that "pleasant words are a honeycomb, sweet to the soul and healing to the bones." These thoughts should be taken to heart and freely shared. The impact of these gestures from others was clearly evident from the tears, smiles, and hugs that flowed from these interactions.

Support Groups

We can't say enough good things about the benefits of participating in support groups. Support groups are for both you and your loved one. They provide a setting that's conducive to sharing, learning, and discovery. It may come as a surprise to learn through support group discussions that some of your challenges and concerns aren't all that unique. As you listen to others, both of you may discover that you face many of the same issues other participants have dealt with or are currently dealing with. A great deal of comfort comes from finding out that neither you nor your loved one are alone in your experiences, concerns, and frustrations.

You'll discover that participating in a support group provides:

- Time for sharing frustrations and experiences
- Opportunities for reassurance and emotional support
- Answers to medical and caregiving questions and options
- Information about available resources
- Suggestions on how to deal with common concerns

From our own experiences and discussions with other caregivers like Patrice, we also know that support groups provide opportunities for developing social connections. In addition, the encouragement and support received might give you the courage and strength to say, "We can do this together."

Many participants have also pointed out that support groups provide an encouraging setting for asking questions and sharing stories without feelings of shame or guilt. There are so many benefits to be gained from support groups. One of the things that quickly becomes apparent when participating in support groups is that there's no way to ask a stupid question. Freedom of expression combined with the knowledge that your input is helping others creates a sense of worth. Having witnessed all of the potential benefits, it concerns us to see people choosing not to participate in these meetings.

In talking with people who are reluctant to participate in support groups, we have learned that they stay away for a variety of reasons. Some are missing out because they don't know about the availability of these groups. Some are shy. Some are private and think, "I don't want anyone knowing anything about my situation." Then again, some are just proudly self-reliant and bravely think that they can do it on their own. They mistakenly think they don't need any help.

However, we found that most of the reasons for staying away and not participating seem to always fall into three categories. First is denial—not wanting to admit that anything is wrong. Second is embarrassment—not being able to publicly admit the possibility of having a terminal diagnosis or a chronic disease. Third is fear—fear of observing others suffering from their same condition and thinking about what may lie ahead for them.

As the caregiver, you can address each of these concerns. Start by having a heart-to-heart discussion with your loved one about the potential benefits of attending a support group. Consider showing them some websites (type in "support groups") that describe the benefits of support groups, or sharing informational fliers found in most doctor's offices. Suggest attending a virtual session and just watching with no pressure to participate.

If you don't think these types of approaches will work, or if they've already failed, then consider another approach. Perhaps someone from your care team, especially a confidant or one of your vitals, might be more successful in starting this conversation with your loved one. Then together, or maybe later when you're alone with your loved one, have an open and frank discussion that encourages an honest exchange of fears, feelings, and emotions.

Gwen and I attended several support groups. Each time we attended as newbies, we found ourselves easing in timidly. However, with each successive meeting, we became a bit more comfortable and open as we discovered we weren't facing unique caregiving challenges. Sure, some things were different for each individual, but we learned from their experiences and then tailored our approach to our specific needs.

For example, early on as I was settling into my caregiving responsibilities, I was faced with a simple task. For several months it had been necessary for me to put in Gwen's studded earrings as she began losing the hand dexterity needed to accomplish this task. I had always thought this task was unique to Gwen's Parkinson's disease. However, it wasn't until I was sitting in a caregiver's support group where we were sharing examples of the tasks we performed for our loved ones that I had an eye-opening moment of awareness.

Two other spouses in the group who were facing different challenges spoke up and said they were also doing the same thing. Just like me, they thought they were the only ones doing this task. After that experience, it didn't take long for me to feel free to open up with fellow caregivers, sharing the things I had learned while seeking their ideas for different approaches to common challenges.

If you or your loved one are still reluctant to attend a support group, at least consider taking a look at some online forums dealing with your particular situation. The following list provides some of the more common gateways for information sources on support groups:

- AARP
- Alzheimer's Association
- American Cancer Society
- American Parkinson Disease Association, Inc.
- American Stroke Association
- Amyotrophic Lateral Sclerosis Association
- The Brain Aneurysm Foundation
- Cleveland Clinics
- The Mayo Clinics

The websites for these national organizations, which are focused on specific diseases and conditions, are good starting points for finding contact information and local support group meeting places, times, and activities. Attendance in these meetings is optional and participation isn't required. By simply attending a group meeting, you can experience the comradery and support that flows from participants who willingly share their experiences, ideas, concerns, frustrations, and joys.

Put aside all imaginable reasons for not attending a support group and please attend at least once. You and your loved one will be pleasantly surprised, if not even amazed, at how enlightening and uplifting these meetings can be.

* * * * *

Pause for Prayer

Dear Lord, as I stop and pray for strength today, help me to remember I am not on my own in taking care of (my loved one). Show me how to reach out and accept the support we need. Let me know who is waiting to step in and help me take care of (my loved one). Help me to remember to not be overwhelmed with all my responsibilities but to stay connected and embrace the love and well-meaning care of others. Thank You that You continue to watch over us. Amen.

CHAPTER NINE

Develop Healthy Habits

*A habit cannot be tossed out the window; it must be
coaxed down the stairs one step at a time.*
Mark Twain

N o one plans to fall off a ladder. It was an accident. Rick
was cleaning the gutter when the ladder slipped out
from under him. One minute everything was fine and
the next minute Cheryl was calling 911. Their lives had suddenly changed. After anxious days in the hospital followed by
months of rehabilitation, they both knew things would never be
the same. Although they had been married for over thirty years
and had always done everything together, working through the
ups and downs was harder than they ever imagined.

When Rick was finally released from rehab, they both knew
that the lingering effects of his brain injury would require many
adjustments to the way they lived. He was still unsteady on his
feet and needed a cane for balance. His speech was slurred. He
had trouble remembering names. He would never drive again.
Buttoning his shirt was now a task and at times he struggled with
cutting up his food. Being together all the time took on a new
meaning; it was 24/7.

Before the accident, they had been looking forward to an early retirement and traveling. Now, with Cheryl quitting her job to take care of Rick, those plans were put on hold. She wanted to be there for him, and he always wanted her to be in his sight. Cheryl was happy to always be by Rick's side, but her friends had started telling her she needed to be thinking about taking care of herself so she could continue taking care of Rick.

The dilemma facing Cheryl is similar to that faced by many intentional caregivers. They know that being there for their loved one is important, but when and how can they be apart? Do any of the following commonly voiced caregiver comments or concerns sound familiar to you?

- "Togetherness is one thing, but never being out of my husband's sight is another thing altogether."
- "I would like to go out for coffee or lunch with my friends, but I would feel guilty leaving my wife home alone for even an hour or two."
- "I can't risk leaving my dad home alone. He might hurt himself or wander off."
- "I really want to go to the women's retreat this weekend, but I know my husband would be anxious the whole time I was gone."
- "I knew it could end up being a 24/7 commitment, but I never thought it would be like this. I never have any time to myself."

If you can relate to any of these statements, it's time to start directing some of your attention to personal self-care or what we call "me time." In order to take care of your loved one, you have to take care of yourself. If this seems like a trivial thought, consider the preflight safety instruction repeated by flight attendants thousands of times each day. Their caution should serve as a vivid reminder of the critical importance of self-care. "If needed, oxygen masks will be released overhead . . . Be sure to secure your own mask before assisting others." The message is clear: if you don't take care of yourself, you may not be able to take care of your loved one.

As the keystone caregiver, falling into predictable daily caregiving routines is easy. Sticking to these established patterns builds reassuring and comforting familiarity. It becomes easy to just keep doing the same things at the same times because this is the way you have always done it. However, it's also easy to begin feeling tied down and potentially becoming less active mentally, physically, and socially. This is what Patrice discovered was happening to herself and what Cheryl's friends noticed was beginning to happen to her. So, what can you do to prevent this from happening?

It Takes Effort

It may take some effort on your part to implement and maintain heathy self-care practices, but there are many things you can do to make this happen. Things like eating right, exercising, having devotional time, drinking plenty of water to stay hydrated, and getting plenty of sleep should be daily practices. Other things like socializing, playing, and having some fun along the way may take a bit more effort to cultivate. However, maintaining these practices provides the strength and reserves needed to be an effective caregiver.

One of the more important healthy habits that may at first seem difficult to develop is finding time to be apart from your loved one. While being available to care for your loved one is a good thing, it is also important to take care of yourself as well.

For some, these opportunities may seem to come naturally. For others, especially those of you who have always done everything together like Rick and Cheryl, it may have to be discussed, agreed to, and deliberately planned. Finding ways to create separation breaks won't be as difficult when your loved one is mobile, capable of being left alone for extended periods of time, and capable of caring for at least some of their own needs. If you are working outside of the home, the act of physically going to work will naturally create some time apart.

However, if you're not working or as your loved one becomes less mobile and more dependent, creating opportunities for separation becomes a necessity, not a luxury. In the immersion and release phases of your journey you can easily become so focused on caregiving that self-care isn't the first thing that pops into your mind. Your intentional caregiving desires will be constantly pushing you to do more and be ever present. This was what Cheryl began to experience as she quit work to care for Rick.

When your loved one can see you or know they can easily call out for you, they feel comfortable knowing you are nearby. They know you are ready, willing, and able to respond to their needs at any time. However, be careful. The need to be ever-present can wear you down. Take time to pace yourself. Don't feel guilty about or shy away from self-care; it isn't being selfish. It's something that's needed and healthy for both of you. In fact, if you've been practicing sitting still with God, you've already experienced a taste of how quiet time equips and strengthens you to face each day.

Other conscious steps to take toward creating separation could be doing something as simple as stepping outside or into another room, enjoying a hobby, or just relaxing for an extended period of time. As you saw in the previous chapter, it could also mean leaving home for even longer breaks. It may take some discussion and effort on your part, but the benefits of these times of separation will be worth the effort. As you become more comfortable with taking breaks, and as your loved one adjusts to you being away, you'll begin to experience some healthy benefits. You'll notice yourself becoming more relaxed and peaceful as the tensions of feeling indispensable begin to fade away.

It may take a great deal of extra effort and ingenuity on your part to create these opportunities for separation. Just like Rick and Cheryl, Gwen and I liked to do things together. We enjoyed each other's company, but we knew how to do things apart from each other. As Gwen's condition continued to deteriorate and we entered the immersion phase of caregiving, she often became anxious when I wasn't around. She needed the reassurance of knowing I was close by if needed. She needed some way to communicate with me when we were not in the same room. At first, she could call out my name; however, when her voice started failing and this method was no longer possible, we needed to improvise and adapt.

We discovered that she could text or call my cell phone when needed. She even went so far as taking her cell phone into the shower, carrying it around her neck in a waterproof scuba diver's pouch. Then, when she could no longer effectively punch the numbers on her phone, we switched to having her use a whistle she kept around her neck.

Finally, when there was no longer enough pucker power for the whistle, we resorted to using small hand bells which were easy to grasp and ring. She kept a bell in the basket on her walker during the day. She also kept one bell in the bedroom, one on the kitchen table, and another one beside her easy chair. We had bells everywhere! By making each of these adaptations, I was able to go about my activities without the fear of being unreachable.

Don't Feel Guilty

Have you asked yourself, "Where and when would I find time in my busy schedule for me time?" Does even the thought of finding me time make you feel a little bit uneasy, if not guilty? Do any of the following thoughts sound familiar?

- "It would be selfish."
- "My loved one needs me."

- "Nobody else can do my job as well as I can."
- "How can I trust someone else with my caregiving duties?"

These and many other guilt-tinged thoughts and questions could undoubtedly weigh on your mind when you begin to consider switching your focus from solely providing care to thinking about the necessity of self-care.

We encourage you to begin making an intentional effort to schedule me time and find at least some small blocks of time focused on meeting your self-care needs. Start out by consistently taking off a couple of hours at a time (once a week or every other week) and then work up to larger blocks of time. Be sure to discuss with your loved one what you're doing and why this time apart is important for both of you. Many caregivers find that they need these breaks once a week, while others tell us every other week is enough for them. But they all tell us how important these breaks are and that taking these breaks helps to keep them energized and positive.

It took time for me to fall into a self-care pattern, but over the years, with a little practice, self-care became a habit. Coordinating these blocks of time became a team effort. As we entered the immersion phase, I found I needed to hire caregivers to stay with Gwen for these breaks every other week for two to four hours. One of her church friends spent two hours each week with her at her Thursday morning women's Bible study. Friends frequently offered to stop by and keep her company while I ran errands. Catherine would drop in for an hour or two each week. After a short visit, I would go into another room to read or slip out to buy groceries. She also scheduled Tuesday afternoon movie sessions with two or three of Gwen's other friends. I used these breaks to run errands, meet with friends, or do things I enjoyed. Sometimes I would even join in on one of the movie sessions with Gwen and the girls, when allowed!

Expand your thinking by exploring other guilt-free opportunities for further me time opportunities. For example, you might consider taking your loved one to an adult day care facility. Many of these facilities are available and offer supervised care, opportunities for social interactions, mental and physical exercises, craft and music programs, assistance with personal care needs, meals, and more. Some programs are available for several hours a day and others are available all day, providing caregivers the peace of mind they need to continue working or to take care of personal business. While Gwen participated in her exercise program, I was able to slip away to a one-hour caregiver's support group meeting that was held in the same building.

Have an Emergency Plan

Being away from your loved one, especially in the latter part of the immersion or release phases, can be stressful for both of you. What if something happened, like your car breaking down or you being in an accident and ending up in the hospital while you were away from home? How would anyone know that you had a loved one at home who was dependent on you for their care?

You can help alleviate some of the guilt and stress of being away by planning ahead to relieve these concerns. If you don't, when a real emergency happens, both of you could suffer!

I thought I had plans to take care of emergencies until I came down with a case of what the doctor finally diagnosed as walking pneumonia. I was so busy caring for Gwen I didn't notice how sick I was. In fact, I'm not sure how this would have ended if Catherine had not stopped by to visit Gwen. As she recalls, when I didn't answer her knock on the door, she decided to come in (we had been texting and she knew the door was unlocked). When she came in, she found me lying on the couch without enough energy to even raise my head. After she got me to sit up, drink some water, and eat some crackers, she offered to sit with Gwen so I could go to an urgent care center. As far as I'm concerned, Catherine's arrival, encouragement, and the care she showed for both of us was nothing short of a miracle. She continued coming by every day for the next three days to help me with basic caregiving chores as I recovered.

Consider carrying an emergency contact card like the one I carried for Gwen, shown below.

In Case of Emergency	I have a Medical Power of Attorney _____ is my designated agent. Cell:	I _____, am the Primary Caregiver for my wife _____. If I am injured contact _____ Cell: _____ to initiate my emergency care plan in _____ County, ____ for her.

Please note, the person designated as your power of attorney on the left-hand side of the card may be the same as or different than the person listed as the primary contact on the right-hand side of the card. In addition, this card indicates you have an emergency plan, along with your county and state of residence. This particular design is sized as a business card to be printed on business card stock, laminated, and then carried in your purse or wallet.

Likewise, in case of an emergency with your loved one at home while you are gone, it would be wise to leave detailed information and instructions posted in a conspicuous place like the refrigerator door. This information should include the names and cell phone numbers for key contacts, detailed care instructions for your loved one including medications, dosages, and times, and an easy-to-follow written emergency plan. In addition, think about having your loved one wear a medical alert bracelet.

I also printed the following information on index cards to allow easier communication for Gwen and others. This was especially helpful when I was taking her to gatherings like her women's Bible study class where I wouldn't be present. As Gwen lost her ability to speak, I found that these index cards helped her to be included in group conversations. I included simple information on the card so she could give it to others as a way of letting them know about her limitations and needs. The following statements might give you some ideas for what types of information the two of you think would be the most meaningful.

Hi, my name is _____.

I have _____ son(s)/daughter(s) and _____ grandchildren.

They live in _____

I have difficulty talking, but love being around people and listening to their conversations.

I like to drink coffee with one cream and one sugar.

My husband's name is _____, and you can reach him at _____.

As you format the cards and fill in the blanks, consider highlighting key words in red for attention grabbing impact. Different cards can also be created for different situations.

Remember, with this level of attention to detail, there's no need to feel guilty while you're apart. It's okay to disconnect from your loved one, to recharge your batteries. Life will still go on even if you're not present to take care of everything. Take time while you're apart to treat yourself to a massage, take long walks, have lunch with a friend, shop, or just run errands.

One caregiver, Jamie, who had young children at home, liked to plan playdates with her kids when her fill-in person was scheduled to care for her husband. She used this time to take her kids to the beach to play, swim, and have a picnic. When her kids were at school, she would take long bike rides. Like Jamie, consider doing something out of the ordinary that will keep you refreshed and energized.

There are many benefits to be derived, other than returning refreshed, from finding and scheduling separation times for both of you. Besides breaking cycles of dependence and feelings of guilt, new opportunities are created for sharing once you are back together again. Begin by sharing what each of you did while apart. Who did you meet, what did you learn, etc.? Ask, "What did you do while I was gone?" These new topics for discussion can also create interest and variety in your lives. You'll be a better caregiver if you're able to not only meet the needs of your loved one, but also your own needs.

Make Exercise a Priority

While me time is essential for your physical and mental well-being, there are many other things you can do together that can be just as beneficial. Exercise and travel are two of these activities. We've experienced them ourselves and often heard others enthusiastically recommend them as well. Both of these activities can be done together, while at the same time affording individual benefits.

When it comes to exercise, have you or your loved one ever made any of the following statements?

- "It's too difficult."
- "It makes me sweat."
- "It takes too much time."
- "It doesn't make any difference."
- "I don't want to do it."
- "I'm just not interested."

The list could go on and on, but enough with the excuses. You know you both need exercise.

Sure, it's only natural for anyone who is aging, dealing with a major injury, or facing a chronic or terminal diagnosis to become more lethargic. Just ask anyone who has been through physical therapy what they think about exercise. They'll tell you, "It hurt, and I didn't want to do it." This reluctance to exercise can happen as early as the recognition and reliance phases of caregiving but becomes even more prevalent during the immersion phase. However, you both need to consciously fight these sedentary tendencies.

When it comes to exercise, make it a priority. Keep moving and strive to never slow down. Medical professionals are quick to say that exercise is one of the best, if not the best, way to enhance quality of life and promote general health. However, before starting any new type of exercise, talk with your doctors and other healthcare professionals to get their suggestions for the best course of action.

Continue or begin exercising now by doing something simple and doing it often. Consider going to a gym, fitness center, or an insurance-sponsored or support group exercise program with your loved one. It often helps to have others around who are dealing with similar situations for inspiration, encouragement, and support. This could also be a good time for both of you to make social contacts. Dance therapy, Tai Chi, yoga, water aerobics, and boxing are just a few types of exercise activities that involve others and can seem more like having fun than doing exercises.

If you already have an exercise routine, keep up the good work! If exercise will be something new, just like everything else we've discussed, start out slowly. Remember, by doing something often it eventually turns it into a habit. Strive to make regular exercise one of your healthy habits. Everyone needs to find ways to exercise, or at least to keep moving as long as physically possible. Consider walking, even if it is only for a short distance. This is one of those exercises that can be either a solitary or a social activity.

148 • REASSURING GUIDANCE

One exercise Gwen and I encountered in almost every exercise group we attended involved having the group form a circle and bounce a beach ball back and forth. I think the highest number of tosses I ever witnessed in a group was forty-five. Shouting, encouragement, laughter, smiles, and fun made this exercise a winner for everyone involved!

Even if your loved one can't go out and exercise with others, you can still help them engage in targeted exercises that can make a difference. Best of all, you don't have to have any special equipment. You can use dumbbells or cans of vegetables for lifting and strengthening. You can use a weight machine, wooden dowels, or PVC pipes (filled with sand if more weight is needed) for stretching and lifting exercises. Once again, the options are limitless. Use your imagination.

If mobility is an issue, there are exercises that can be performed in a chair—yes, even a wheelchair. For example, you can toss a ball back and forth like we did in our support group. It can be lifted over your head and moved from side to side while holding it with both hands. It can also be placed between your knees for squeezing exercises to build additional strength. The same types of exercises can be accomplished with resistance bands. Once again, if mobility is an issue, consider load-bearing exercises like standing, squatting, and rising up on the toes (for safety reasons, you may need to assist by holding a gait belt). Don't let your loved one's condition be a detriment to exercise.

Also consider swimming, which is excellent for stretching, as well as an aerobic workout. If you or your loved one can't swim, then at least get them in the pool so they can feel the freedom of walking or movement. Water provides a great deal of support and its natural resistance when moving encourages exercise with seemingly little effort. If either of you have a fear of water, stay in the shallow end and use flotation devices that can relieve those fears by holding the person upright while doing water exercise routines.

Pool noodles and aquatic fitness devices are just two examples of commonly used flotation devices. I once noticed a mother putting an exercise flotation device on her young son and then moving him from his wheelchair into the swimming pool. Although he couldn't use his legs and the other children stared at first, they quickly forgot about his limitation as he stroked his way over and joined in their games. Thank God for those caregivers who make a difference through their thoughtful actions.

It's easy to take a large standard pool noodle and shape it into a circle for a do-it-yourself safety flotation ring that can be placed over the head and under the arms. I did this at the recommendation of another caregiver and was able to let Gwen exercise while I swam some laps. I have now passed this simple water exercise hack on to more people than I can even remember.

There are exercise programs for every level of ability, and many are sponsored by non-profits and hospitals. There is also professional help that can be accessed through occupational and physical therapists, as well as personal trainers. The following exercise ideas are provided to get your thinking started; you can easily add to these ideas as you consider your loved one's abilities and limitations:

- If you can walk, walk
- If you can swim, swim
- If you can lift any type of weights, lift them
- If you can stretch, stretch
- If you can ride a bike, even if it is stationary, ride it
- If you can push a wheelchair around the block, push it
- If you can do it together, do it together
- You get the picture; you just need to do it!

The resources you can tap into are amazing. All you need to do is ask around. No matter what level of ability you or your loved one possess, there is some type of exercise both of you can do. There are programs designed to improve agility, balance, cardiovascular health, endurance, strength, and much more. Find the one that works for you and your loved one.

The Benefits of Travel

Now here's an activity that can be healthy both physically and mentally. If you ever doubt or question the benefits of travel, all you need to do is look at the media coverage for trips made possible by *Make a Wish* and other similar charitable organizations. The excitement, smiles, and pure joy seen on the faces of terminally ill children and their grateful families should be all the evidence you need for the positive impacts of travel.

I speak from experience. Gwen and I traveled extensively, often accompanied by family and friends, who were always willing to lend a helping hand. Even after she entered the immersion phase of caregiving and became restricted to a wheelchair, we continued to travel. We never considered her condition or the wheelchair to be a deterrent as we traveled literally all over the United States and other places around the world. You can do it, too! You might not be as adventuresome as we were, but think about the opportunities. It just requires a little bit of extra advanced planning.

Although you may consider travel to be out of the question due to financial or physical constraints, we encourage you to at least consider the possibilities. Travel is a great way to battle boredom and provides the stimulus to be both positive and forward looking. It could be doing something as simple as visiting friends and relatives, spending time at a nearby hotel, or arranging for a few days just to get away.

Travel doesn't need to involve exotic places in distant locations. Planning trips can be almost as fun as taking them. Planning for and taking a staycation can be just as fun and refreshing as a major getaway. Consider the possibility of making reservations at a nearby bed and breakfast, hotel, or resort and having a ride share service pick you up and whisk you away. If you aren't constrained by time, you can search the internet for reservations during slow times (this varies by location) and find some great bargains.

When you arrive, you could go out to dinner and a movie, the theater, the zoo, a museum, or . . . (you fill in the blank). If you think getting out of your room and out on the town would be difficult, then choose a hotel with room service and pick an in-room movie from their selection. You may even want to look for a hotel with an indoor pool and sneak in a little stretching exercise on the side.

We also encourage you to seriously consider an often over-looked option for adventure and respite care combined in one location: cruising. Would you like to have your bed made up for you every day, have all of your meals prepared and served, and have a variety of entertainment options to choose from, all in a relaxing atmosphere? If this sounds enticing, seriously think about taking a cruise.

We heard so many wonderful stories from people in caregiving relationships who had cruised and loved it, just like Gwen and I did. It's a personal experience in being pampered that can't be beat! You may have to save up to do it once in your lifetime or you may find after one experience that you can figure out a way to do it more often.

Cruising may also provide opportunities to spend quality time with family and friends. Having friends and loved ones close by, as well as a staff accustomed to dealing with people who have physical challenges, can be a blessing for everyone. Cruises offer opportunities for everyone to select from a menu of activities, excursions, and entertainment options to fit their abilities and interests. Even sitting on the deck and watching people, the views, and other shipboard activities can be an enjoyable change of pace. Then over meals, discussing plans for the day or recapping the day's experiences creates shared memories. There is even a doctor on board, so check your worries and concerns at the dock and get aboard.

Thinking About Major Life Changes

The next chapter deals with what may seem like disheartening realities to be faced in the release phase of your journey. Even if caregiving is a temporary bump in the road or if you find yourself in the early phases of your caregiving journey, we encourage you to at least scan the topics covered in the next chapter. That way you'll be able to discuss some of the decisions you and your loved one will need to make while clear thinking and communication are still possible. If you're well along in your caregiving journey and into the immersion phase, then you'll probably need to read, think about, and earnestly discuss some of these hard choices.

You might be asking yourself, "How will I know if I am deep into the immersion phase of caregiving?" The answer can probably be summed up by saying that you've become constantly hypervigilant. You're always anxious, never far away from your loved one, and always looking and listening intently for any noticeable changes in their behavior.

You might also find yourself constantly checking your phone for text messages or missed calls when you're separated, even though you know you would've felt the buzz or heard the ping. In other words, you're constantly on edge, instinctively knowing that a major change or health event is imminent.

This is the time to be praying and asking God for the strength needed to cope with making difficult end-of-life decisions. Begin thinking about when the timing will be right and who should be included in these discussions. Remember, God will be right beside you and continue to guide you and hold you close to Him. Don't wait until you're overwhelmed to ask for God's help. You don't have to handle these decisions on your own. Whatever you face, you face with God. Genesis 26:24 says, "Do not be afraid, for I am with you."

* * * * *

Pause for Prayer

Dear Lord, as I turn to You in prayer today, please take away all of my lingering concerns and fears about our future. As we move forward, help me to be aware of the need to take care of myself so that I can take care of (my loved one). Open my mind for ways to create a healthy balance of fun, exercise, and adventure in our lives. Help us to continue to trust You. Amen.

CHAPTER TEN

Plan for the Inevitable

God gave us memory so that we might have roses in
December.
J. M. Barrie

I don't know about you, but I don't like saying goodbye. It's always been hard for me, especially when saying goodbye to family members, relatives, and close friends who've traveled for a visit. An intense feeling of emptiness engulfs me as we hug, wave, and say goodbye. Then, as this empty feeling of sadness slowly ebbs away, unanswerable questions begin creeping in. How had our time together gone by so fast? Was there anything we'd forgotten to talk about? When would we see each other again?

Why is it that those whom we treasure so much touch our hearts so deeply? As you near the end of your caregiving journey, many of these same emotional feelings and questions can surface. Try as you might to hold on to your loved one, the time comes when the inevitable can't be avoided. Ready or not, when the end arrives, as heartbreaking as it feels, you have to say goodbye and let go.

The first glimmer of this coming reality emerged on Gwen's last wellness exam. The doctor made a notation in her file that

155

I had never seen before: "Medically fragile." Shortly thereafter, a member of our support group said, "Have you explored how hospice could help?" She was noticing something I couldn't see or didn't want to see. I had advised other people to explore the benefits of hospice but had never considered these services for ourselves.

I was strong and independent. Some would even say I was stubborn. I knew I could take care of our needs. I had a good support network. My wife wasn't dying; I didn't need any help from hospice. I was in denial. Finally, one of my confidants got my attention by asking me to think about what Gwen might need in the way of extra comfort and care. She urged me to at least visit with someone from hospice.

Hesitantly, I stopped by the local hospice office. The person who greeted me explained that I would need to schedule a home visit so Gwen's condition could be evaluated. When I got home, I told Gwen that I didn't think she was ready for hospice care, but I would like to schedule a visit to learn more about what they had to offer. I made the call to make an appointment for the next Friday afternoon. That's when the wheels started turning. An appointment was actually made for the very next day. I was surprised they could come so soon. My head was spinning, but reality began setting in when she said, "We'll have someone there at 9:00 a.m. tomorrow."

We were anxious about this visit, but felt prepared. I had already read all I could about hospice care on the internet. In addition, Gwen and I had discussed her final wishes months before and had completed all of the necessary medical and legal forms. However, since we weren't completely sure about what to expect, I asked Catherine if she would be with us during the visit. I knew she had walked with others through the hospice experience and would know what to expect and what questions to ask. With a good friend by our side, we were at least mentally prepared when the intake staff from hospice arrived.

After just a few basic questions, they recommended that Gwen be placed under hospice care. When the lead person asked if this would be okay with us, we were shocked. This was all happening way too fast! After a few speechless moments, I looked over at Gwen and could see the fear and tears in her eyes. The room was quiet. No one said a word. We looked deeply in each other's eyes. Even though no words were spoken, we both knew the time was right for this emotionally painful move.

It seemed like time stood still until we finally nodded in agreement. The hospice worker asked to see a copy of Gwen's living will. This is where we ran into a problem. In the past, Gwen could verbally indicate that she authorized me to make medical decisions on her behalf. However, since she had reached a point where she could no longer speak, she couldn't verbally indicate her consent for me to make this decision for her. I explained how we communicated through nods and blinks and asked if this would suffice. The answer was no: she had to give a verbal consent.

The agent listed on her living will would have to authorize her admission into hospice care. Gwen had designated our son, Chad, as her authorized agent. So, hospice called him. He didn't answer. I explained that he wouldn't answer a call from an unknown number and asked if I could call and ask him to answer the phone if she tried again. She said that would be fine as long as I didn't explain anything about the call he would be receiving. This time Chad answered the call from a stranger who said, "This is hospice. You are listed on Gwen Cook's living will as her agent. Do you authorize us to put her under hospice care?"

He said, "Yes."

I called him after the appointment was over to explain what was happening. He told me he was surprised by the call, but luckily, he knew he had been listed as the contact person on the document. It had been an emotionally draining morning, but it was such a blessing that Catherine had been with us. We sat together after the appointment and talked about all that had happened. We both made sure that our conversation was focused on Gwen. Then, before she left, she asked us to all hold hands as she offered up a prayer seeking God's comfort and guidance for us during this anxiety-filled time.

No matter how much you mentally plan and prepare for the inevitable finality, you'll never be completely prepared. However, the more planning and preparation you do before entering the release phase of your journey, the more peace of mind you'll experience during these final months, weeks, and days. We know from our experiences that you'll benefit from the support that comes from your care team now more than ever before. Discussing and working through the issues presented in this chapter should be another team effort involving you, the person you are caring for, and those vitals and confidants who have always been there for you.

Even with this level of support, you'll be emotionally challenged. It will be a time for gathering every ounce of courage you can muster. It will be a time to come to grips with discussing and making final decisions about personal topics with someone you love.

Everyone reacts differently during these highly emotional discussions. Catherine reminded me how she noticed this when watching friends deal with these stressful conversations. We both agreed that I remained stoic, while Ken approached the situation matter-of-factly. Julie was almost pleading as she reached out for help, and Lara seemed to be in a state of shock.

If you think you're ready to begin, let's get started. By the time you get to the release phase of your journey, you will probably already feel like you've been on what seems like an emotionally and physically draining rollercoaster ride. You will have experienced times filled with pleasant memories you will always cherish. There will be other times you would just as soon forget. You hung on tight through the twists and turns of all of these experiences and now you find yourself on that decelerating coast that always comes at the end of the ride.

Instead of looking back on all the things you and your loved one have been through, it may be more helpful to deal with present issues and think about the future. As you try to imagine what the future holds while dealing with the hustle and bustle of caregiving, close your eyes for a moment. Take in a deep breath, exhale; then think about the beauty, warmth, and glow of a softly burning candle. Now, keep that image in mind as you start thinking about preparing for the end of your caregiving journey.

Preparation

Whether you wanted to or not, you've been watching your loved one's candle burn the whole time you've been on this journey. When your journey first started, it may have seemed that if both of you tried your best, you could make it go on forever. However, just as you know that a candle can't burn forever, deep down inside, you knew, both mentally and emotionally, that your loved one wouldn't be with you forever. You knew that sooner or later they would be passing into God's loving arms.

As you near the end of the release phase of your journey, your loved one, just like the flame on a candle, slowly starts fading away. As the flame starts to fade, you can tend to it, trying to coax it to burn a little longer by trimming the wick and pouring off excess wax. As the end nears for your loved one, you'll be just as diligent, if not more so, in doing everything possible to keep them as part of your life. However, as the end approaches, you realize there's nothing you can do to keep the candle burning or to keep your loved one with you.

Hopefully, with the pleasant image of a candle's gently flickering flame resting comfortably in your mind, you can prepare yourself to begin thinking about making some difficult but necessary decisions. Please be aware that we've never experienced or talked with anyone, no matter how confident they appeared to be, who was fully prepared to make these end-of-life related decisions. Just thinking about and discussing these decisions will probably bring a lump to your throat and tears to your eyes. So, you may want to have a tissue ready before we go any further.

Let's begin by looking at some basic tasks that need to be completed and choices that need to be made. Then we'll move on to more complex and emotional decisions. It might be easiest to think about these basic tasks and choices as mechanical decisions, approaching them as items on a checklist. That way, after coming to agreement on a topic, finding and/or completing a document, and placing it in a safe location, you can check it off your list. You'll get a nice sense of accomplishment. This won't happen in a day or even a week, so leave plenty of time for sorting through both paperwork and emotions. It's challenging enough when these discussions involve a spouse, but they can be even more challenging if they involve family members or close friends who are depending on you for the majority of their care.

Legal and Financial Issues

The list of decisions and documents that need to be completed may seem daunting at first. However, just like with everything else you've faced in your caregiving journey, if help is needed, it's never far away. We've talked with several people who've successfully assembled and completed all of these documents on their own. However, it's important to note that if you decide on preparing do-it-yourself legal documents, make sure they're current and appropriate for the state in which you live. I felt confident completing and arranging all of these documents, but I was also encouraged to at least have a lawyer review them. I did this and was delighted and relieved when she said everything was in order.

We've also talked with other people who said they'd never attempt to complete these documents on their own. They relied on the professional advice and assistance of accountants, financial planners, and lawyers. In these stressful times, it may be tempting to make quick or emotional decisions when seeking professional advice for completing these important documents. Do your research, using the same approach you did when searching for medical professionals to add to your caregiving team. Don't engage the services of someone who's not a specialist in these matters. Ask for referrals, check references, look for ratings when available, and identify those who are leaders in their field. Most importantly, though, find someone you trust.

It's not our intention to provide legal or financial advice. However, it is our desire to at least provide enough information to get you started. The first set of decisions you'll need to make involves legal and estate documents (see Appendix A: Legal and Estate Documents). The second set of decisions focuses on financial issues (see Appendix B: Financial Accounts). The third and final set of decisions consists of making sure all other important documents are in order (see Appendix C: Other Important Documents).

Whether it's been you or your loved one paying the bills and attending to the finances, make sure the appropriate survivor's name is on all accounts, bank cards (debit/credit), insurance policies, vehicle titles, deeds, etc., as needed. Prepare a list of all automatic payments, so these can be stopped. Then place all of these documents in an electronic file or in one physical location where they can be easily accessed. The physical location should be somewhere other than a safe deposit box. If your loved one's name is on the safe deposit box rental agreement form, you may not have access to it until after the death certificate is filed.

In addition, let someone you trust (it could be your accountant, lawyer, brother, sister, child, etc.) know where these documents are stored. Also make sure they have the combinations to locks, know where keys are kept, and the location of passwords to access online accounts and/or documents. Finally, don't overlook social media accounts. They'll need passwords to access these accounts and instructions on how they are to be memorialized (closed).

Life Care Choices

Now, let's move on to what can be far more emotional decisions than those basic, mechanical ones you just made surrounding legal and financial issues: life care choices. There may come a time when you realize you can no longer independently care for your loved one without assistance. What type of caregiving services will you need? Can you stay where you currently live, or will one or both of you need to move into some type of assisted living, nursing, or memory care facility? What will you do if the person you're caring for doesn't want to move? These are weighty questions that call for prayer and time to listen for God's guidance and reassurance.

For most of us, our first choice would be to stay where we consider home for as long as possible. This makes sense as familiar surroundings can provide a feeling of comfort and security. Staying where you consider home could also be less expensive. In addition, the more caregiving functions you can do yourself or get others to help with, the more money you can save. Saving money may become critical in the long run, as expanding needs may necessitate hiring professional in-home care staff or having to place your loved one in a full-time care facility. This was on my mind as I began weighing our options. Would I be able to find the help needed to keep Gwen at home, or at some point would we need to consider moving her into an assisted living facility? How much would each of these alternatives cost, and where would Gwen be the most comfortable?

If you've ever been around someone in their waning years and months, you know how disturbing it can be for them to suddenly find themselves being placed in new and unfamiliar surroundings. In fact, changes in surroundings can be so upsetting that when you know this disruption to the norm is inevitable, you should start planning as far in advance as possible for when, where, and how these needed changes can be met. Planning for and discussing these moves ahead of time allows your loved one to adjust to the idea of being uprooted—and to become comfortable with the idea of being cared for somewhere away from home.

If you and your loved one decide that staying at home is your preferred choice, there may be some additional considerations that need to be addressed. Will you be hiring part-time or full-time caregivers? Will you find them yourself or will you be using an agency? Could a family member or relative move in at some time in the future to provide assistance? Will whoever ends up helping need their own private bedroom? Should they be compensated for their time? If so, how much should they be paid—or can some other form of in-kind compensation, such as the transfer of title to real estate or personal assets, be arranged?

If you're thinking about having a family member or relative step in to help, what would this arrangement look like? If both you and your loved one are considering moving in with a family member or relative, have you discussed what this move might involve? Have you thought about drawing up a written agreement outlining the details of the arrangement to avoid future misunderstandings?

When Gwen's father passed away, there was no question that her mother, Linnie, wouldn't be able to live on her own. She was adamant about not moving into an assisted living facility. All eight of their children, with the exception of Margaret, lived hundreds of miles away. Everyone just assumed Linnie would move in with Margaret, her husband Harold, and their two boys. However, there were two problems. Neither of their houses were big enough for the five of them, and there was a question of fairness. Was it fair for everyone to just assume Margaret should take on the sole responsibility of caring for Linnie?

Finally, Harold, sensing some of the tensions and unspoken concerns, proposed a win-win solution. Linnie could sell her home, they could sell their home, and with the proceeds they could buy a larger home. However, he insisted on one condition. When Linnie passed away, he and Margaret would inherit the house. He was bold enough to say that this seemed only fair since Margaret would be the one physically caring for their aging mother. Although there was some reluctance, everyone finally agreed to this arrangement. The idea worked, and Linnie was able to live out her final years surrounded by family.

If a decision is made to not stay at home, what type of assisted living facility will you want your loved one to live in? Will it need to be a facility with room for one or two people? Facilities, services, and options can vary widely, ranging all the way from supported independent living arrangements to 24/7 skilled nursing and comprehensive memory care services.

If the move involves you and your loved one, consider the option of living in an assisted living facility that has progressive services to accommodate both of your needs. That way you'll have access to common facilities like restaurants, gyms, social activity centers, and on-call medical assistance. As more care is needed, transfers can be arranged at the same facility. Care can progress from independent living options that include light housekeeping and meals with on-call nursing assistance to a setting with more supervised care. Finally, when 24/7 care is needed, a move can be arranged into another part of the facility where full-time supervision and professional nursing care are provided.

My friends, Debbie and Ron, discovered how much easier life was when they decided to move together to a nearby assisted living facility. Ron was beginning to have memory issues, so Debbie decided that they should make the move while he could still help with decision making. She told us how glad she was that they made the decision when they did. She knew she needed full-time help to take care of Ron, but she also knew she needed to remain active. She now has a sense of peace knowing that Ron is getting the care he needs, and they can still enjoy social activities and meals together without ever leaving the facility.

Selecting the best care facility may seem overwhelming. However, this task can be made easier by developing a short list of acceptable facilities. Then, with your loved one, visit these chosen facilities to agree on the best possible choice(s). If you don't plan on making an immediate move, at least get on the waiting list, as your preferred choice may not have immediate openings.

Hospice Care

Your loved one's final days and hours may happen at home, in a hospital, or in an assisted living facility. No matter where it happens, you have an opportunity to make a difference. Don't wait like I did to benefit from the loving care and attention provided through hospice services. Just hearing, saying, or even thinking about hospice (or palliative) care can be scary. However, consider looking into how these services can assist both you and your loved one in this special time of need.

Hospice (or palliative) care can be provided to anyone suffering from a serious accident or life-threatening illness. However, it is not typically rendered until a person is considered to be in their final stage of life. In some cases, we have seen people who have been under hospice care graduate out of it as their conditions improved, at least temporarily. Hospice will in no way shorten your loved one's life.

So, don't be afraid to explore what these options have to offer. If you are stepping in from the outside as a care team member, don't be timid about suggesting hospice care if you feel God nudging you to do so. These programs are staffed with an amazing group of people who can become an integral part of the care team. There will be a team manager, a doctor, a nurse, a nurse's aide, a chaplain, a social worker, a volunteer, and in some locations even a musician. They've all been specially trained and have a calling to deal with death and end-of-life decisions and are always available to answer your questions.

The hospice team's knowledge of nutrition, medical equipment, supplies, and how to make your loved one comfortable, as well as their ability to explain what is happening can be a great source of comfort and encouragement. Our experiences have shown that they strive to be more like family than simply medical professionals. They can be a beautiful blessing by providing an extra layer of caregiving services, including respite care and emotional support, as you deal with many personal and stressful decisions.

In addition, you'll get added spiritual support when you let your team members know you are people of faith. They aren't allowed to initially talk about how faith has impacted their lives unless you bring up the subject first. On every occasion, once the topic has been broached we've seen how talk of God's faithfulness, promises, and love fill their conversations. Gwen always looked forward to hearing their stories of hope and peace while receiving their comforting care. This special level of care was especially apparent when the hospice musician came to see Gwen and sang her favorite songs. Knowing this meant so much to Gwen, I invited other people to come and be with us whenever the musician was scheduled to visit. Having friends join us in listening to and singing their favorite songs made it easy for everyone to be together in a joyous way.

Letting Go

Letting go is the hardest part of saying goodbye. It is much different than saying goodbye when you head to the store. It is the deep, deep recognition that there'll never be any more welcome home greetings. It is the reality of permanent physical separation from your loved one until you meet again in heaven. Just thinking about the possibility of being permanently separated from your loved one can be upsetting.

Have you thought about how you'll let go of a friend or loved one who is so very close to you? Faith teaches us that death is a natural part of life. It's helpful to remember John 14:1–3, where Jesus says, "Do not let your heart be troubled. Trust in God, trust also in me. In my Father's house are many rooms; if it were not so, I would have told you. I am going there to prepare a place for you. And if I go and prepare a place for you, I will come back and take you to be with me that you also may be where I am." This is the promise of a place in heaven that Jesus is preparing for each of us who believe in Him and accept Him as our Savior. When you're both people of faith, you can rest assured that heaven awaits you and that you'll see each other again.

It may help to become more comfortable with thoughts of death, dying, and what it means to go to heaven by thinking about a story Catherine Marshall conveyed in her book, *Beyond Ourselves*. In it, she explains death and heaven by telling an easily understood, down-to-earth story about an exhausted young boy who falls asleep in his mom's bed and then wakes up later in another place, his own bed.

The mother asks her son to remember when, as a child, he would sometimes be so tired at night that he couldn't even undress himself and find his way to bed. She reminds him how he would just tumble into her bed and fall asleep. In the morning, he would be so surprised to wake up and find himself in his own bed, in his own room. While you slept, his mother explains, you were moved there. That's what death is like. You'll just wake up one morning to find yourself enjoying a new life in heaven because God, who loves you so much, has taken you there.

Helping a person die with grace is one of the most significant privileges you can experience in life. When the time comes to accept the difficult reality of death, you'll need to summon the courage to tell your loved one that it is okay for them to let go (die). You have taken care of them physically. Now they are looking to you for reassurance that it is okay to let go of their earthly struggles. This is a time for reassuring them that they have fought valiantly and that it is okay to no longer put their energy into fighting just to stay alive. This is the time to tell them how much they are loved by you and others. Let them know you'll be okay without them. Remind them of God's promise that you will be reunited in heaven.

After a brave fifteen-year struggle with the obvious effects of Parkinson's disease, the time came to let Gwen go. When the hospice nurse told me I needed to do this, I told her I couldn't and kept asking her to do it for me. She would always say, "This is something I can't do for you. You have to tell Gwen that you give her permission to let go and die. She loves you so much that she'll keep hanging on because she doesn't want to hurt you."

After many, many prayers, I finally found the courage to hold her hands, look into her eyes and give her my permission to die. Even as the tears streamed down our faces, I could see a sense of peace settling across Gwen's face and knew the nurse was right.

Soon the hospice nurse told me Gwen only had a few days to live. She also said I should alert anyone who needed to say goodbye to her. It was excruciatingly agonizing to decide when I should call our son, Chad, and daughter-in-law, Sabrina. We had just finished an extremely difficult road trip to be with them on Mother's Day a few weeks before. The company Chad worked for had just been purchased and he was flying to different locations helping with the transition. Since he had recently hugged his mother goodbye, I anguished over when and how I should share this disturbing news with him.

I called Sabrina, and in between bursts of crying, shared the news with her, seeking her input on when to tell Chad. I didn't want him to feel like I was laying a guilt trip on him to be with us, but I didn't want to sugar coat the situation either. After a lot of prayer and discussion, she finally convinced me to call him and let the decision be his on whether or not to come. Summoning up every bit of courage I could find, I touched his number on my phone. Before he could answer, I started crying. In between sobs, I was able to tell him that if he wanted to tell his mom goodbye he would need to get here in the next couple of days. It's a good thing I made that call. His new boss told him to go, and he was on the next plane to his home. Then he and Sabrina immediately drove over 1,100 miles straight through to be with us the very next day!

We had two days to say our goodbyes and I-love-yous. This was a time filled with tears, exchanging knowing glances, listening to Gwen's favorite Christian music, reading Scripture, saying prayers, holding hands, and sharing soft gentle touches. I was sad, but at the same time filled with joy to have us all together as family. It was a pleasant Sunday evening in June when we could all sense the end was near. The windows were open to let in fresh air, and we had gathered on her bed, touching and loving on her. At 9:30 that evening, Gwen breathed her last breath.

All was quiet until the moment she passed away. Then, at that exact moment, we heard a whole chorus of birds singing in a tree outside our bedroom window. It was pitch black outside. It wasn't just one or two birds singing, but all different kinds of birds, singing their cheerful mixture of beautiful melodies for several minutes. As we held hands and each of us said a prayer, there was no question in our minds: we knew their chorus was heralding her ascension into heaven! God had filled us with His peace (Romans 15:13).

Details, Details

With death, you'll experience the ultimate shock, a devastating realization of separation. There will be deep and painful sadness. Your pastor, vitals, constants, friends, and family members can be especially helpful at this time. They can listen to your concerns, console you, guide you, and provide the prayers and spiritual support needed to get through the shock of loss. Soak in these expressions of love, sympathy, and comfort, letting them surround you like a warm blanket on a cold winter night.

As difficult as it may seem, in this time of shock and grief, you'll need to think about funeral arrangements. All of these decisions were simplified for me, as Gwen had definitely stated some of her desires. She knew which pastor she wanted to conduct her service, she knew that she wanted to be cremated, and she knew that she wanted "Amazing Grace" sung at her service. There were still questions, but everything became a whole lot easier when we arrived at the funeral home. To my surprise, we discovered that the owner and Chad had gone to high school together. Although he was not personally involved in any of the arrangements, it was comforting knowing that he knew us. It was another reminder of God's presence and continuing care for us.

It was very different for my friend Kanesha when her husband Rashon passed away. Since they had not talked about his final wishes, she struggled with knowing what to do. She knew she had to make these arrangements, but she wasn't emotionally up to the task. In fact, it was her sister who stepped in and called two nearby funeral homes. The different costs, questions about an open or a closed casket, cremation or burial, levels of service, and other options were mind-boggling. Knowing there were difficult choices to make and more options to explore, she asked her pastor for guidance. After their discussions, her sister then went with her to the funeral home they selected to make the final arrangements. During this emotionally devastating time, Kanesha said, "I needed my pastor and sister to lean on when I was a total wreck."

Don't put yourself in this type of situation. Start thinking and talking about funeral arrangements sooner rather than later. When death finally arrives, you'll be torn with conflicting emotions. You'll be devastated, but at the same time you'll take comfort in knowing your loved one's suffering is over. It is difficult at a time like this to also be thinking about making funeral arrangements. Hopefully you'll have already asked your loved one how they would like to be remembered and honored.

Since funeral or memorial services provide opportunities for people to gather, share stories, and celebrate life, ask your loved one how they want their service conducted. Ask them if they want a small, intimate funeral service or a large celebration of life.

Having discussed these and other questions (see Appendix D: Funeral Planning Questions) can relieve some of the stresses encountered during these emotionally draining and trying times. Thinking about the importance of all the available options lets you decide what must be done, what might be nice to do, and what's not really important. Prepaid funeral policies/contracts may be very helpful in taking away some of the decision making burdens, as well as relieving financial concerns.

In addition to a funeral service, you may also want to consider other ways of finding closure and saying your last goodbyes. It could be a reception for family and friends, a gathering at your home, a time of reflection in a room at the funeral home, a graveside service, or the scattering of your loved one's ashes. However you decide to find closure, take time to embrace, cherish, and share your memories. With so many decisions to make, your pastor can be especially helpful, comforting and guiding you along the way. You can also find helpful support and suggestions through hospice and the funeral home.

The process of discussing what to include in an obituary memorializing your loved one's life can also help in bringing closure to their death. Reviewing or discussing what to include becomes a time for remembrances. Deciding which special accomplishments, people, and events to include creates an opportunity to share these memories with those who are mourning with you. Processing these thoughts and putting them in writing can be a small step forward in the process of healing.

Going to the funeral home and touching your loved one's casket or picking up their cremated remains will engulf you with a personal feeling of ultimate sadness that no one else will ever understand. Open up and let the tears flow; let them flow, and flow, and flow. Give yourself time and space to process these feelings and everything that has happened. The devastating shock of death, along with the activities and people associated with saying goodbye, are emotionally draining.

As you face the details of making new decisions and choices, don't be hasty. Try to avoid making any critical decisions during and following this time of loss and heightened emotional stress. You'll be emotionally vulnerable, so wait as long as possible—maybe even a year or two—before doing anything that can't be easily reversed or undone. Things like selling a home, moving to another city, remarrying, or giving away or selling possessions could easily lead to later regrets. This is a good time to lean on your confidants or vitals and at least discuss any plans you're contemplating before taking action.

Remember God's faithfulness and promises to always walk with you and be with you. He will continue to comfort, sustain, and strengthen you as you find yourself needing to let go and say goodbye to your loved one. When the time comes, He will help you release your loved one into His eternal care.

* * * * *

Pause for Prayer

Dear Lord, thank You that You are with us and that we are not alone as we find ourselves having to say goodbye to each other. Knowing that (my loved one) will pass into Your loving arms at the end of this journey gives me the reassurance that I can confidently release him/her into Your eternal care. Thank You that You will continue to comfort me and keep me close to You. Amen.

CHAPTER ELEVEN

Healing After Loss

Hope is the thing with feathers that perches in the soul—and sings the tunes without the words—and never stops at all.
Emily Dickinson

Even before death arrived, you may have begun reflecting on where life had brought you and what lay ahead. You probably feel exhausted, depleted, worn out, and even overwhelmed. You've been deeply involved in the everyday tasks of caregiving, but now, with death, there's a void in your life. You may be questioning why God has allowed so many challenges and changes to happen in your life. You may be asking, "What is next for me?"

As the well-wishers who gathered to comfort you at your time of loss return to their lives, a profound quietness begins to settle in. There's a sense of emptiness. The bed is empty, the chair at the table is empty, you don't have to be vigilant anymore, and you realize the routines of your life will never be the same. You'll no longer be able to experience the reassuring presence and warmth of your loved one. You're at a loss for how to fill this emptiness and how to spend your time. Although your caregiving responsibilities are over, your life's journey isn't over. It's just changing. You find yourself needing a new sense of direction.

In these times of questioning and soul-searching, reach out to God through prayer. Ask Him for guidance, comfort, and peace. Rest in the assurance that He is with you during these unsettled times. Just thinking about the promises found in the familiar hymn "Great Is Thy Faithfulness" can be comforting. The hymn reminds us that God's compassion and faithfulness are new every morning. He provides for everything we need: strength, hope, and peace. "Continue to live in God, rooted and built up in Him, strengthened in the faith" (Colossians 2:6–7).

Now, maybe more than ever, it may be helpful to focus your attention on me time as you begin searching for a new balance in your life. This is a time to do things that will restore your heart, soul, and mind. This is a time to be with people who can provide judgment-free listening ears and much-needed hugs. This is your opportunity to relax, free from expectations. For me, walking alone or with friends through the woods, soaking in the beauty of God's creation, gave me a newfound sense of balance. I also found that taking long, uninterrupted afternoon naps restored my strength. What can you do to restore your heart, soul, and mind?

Relaxing and freely talking about and reflecting on the past can open the door to thinking about the future. Don't feel rushed to make decisions and move on. Take time to grieve, process your loss, and most importantly, fill yourself with a sense of peace and hope. Trust God and do not be afraid. The Lord is your strength and song (Isaiah 12:2). Your life is still in God's hands.

Grieving

With death comes grieving; there is no avoiding it. It's an important part of letting go and beginning your road to healing. Take comfort in knowing that where there's deep grief, there was great love.

If you're an emotional person, outward grieving will come naturally. If, on the other hand, you're stoic, you may attempt to hold grieving at arm's length. No matter how expressive or reserved you are, your initial grief can consume you in what may seem like a tsunami of emotions.

You may struggle to deal with this flood of emotions, seemingly gasping for air as you try to find the surface and begin to bring balance into your life. Don't be surprised at how easily you find yourself crying. In our experiences, everyone we know who has lost a loved one has cried no matter how strong they thought they were. The uncontrollable torrents of painful sobbing can be long and intense.

For days, months, and even years, you may cry for what seems like no apparent reason. At Gwen's funeral, I became visibly aware of how this uncontrollable reaction could sweep over people. I'd put a lot of tissues in my pockets, knowing that I'd be crying. I certainly used a few of them, but I ended up passing out all the rest to well-wishers in the receiving line after the funeral. It seemed like every time I touched someone's hand who had lost a spouse, no matter how long ago, they began crying as they shared my grief and reexperienced their own grief.

You won't ever completely get over losing a loved one. However, no matter how painful your separation, life goes on. You'll start to improve moving forward. What will moving forward look like? Well, I decided to write a book about caregiving. Bob planted a tree in memory of his wife, Linda. Carolina decided to volunteer at the local soup kitchen to honor the memory of her mother. What will you decide to do in honor of your loved one? You may want to start a new hobby, learn a new skill, travel, or . . . (you fill in the blank).

Remember, in this time of grieving and emotional healing, you're not alone. God has promised to walk with you and be with you to comfort, sustain, and strengthen you. Deuteronomy 33:27 says, "God is our refuge." God is trustworthy in all times and in

178 • REASSURING GUIDANCE

all situations. Psalm 18:2 says, "The Lord is my rock, my fortress, and my deliverer. My God is my rock in whom I take refuge. He is my shield and my stronghold."

Research on grieving shows that it's nothing new or mysterious. It's a process that has been studied and restudied numerous times. You can open up any book, read any article, or look on the internet to find websites on the grieving process and you're sure to see a discussion of the five classical stages of grieving: denial, anger, bargaining, depression, and acceptance (Kubler-Ross).

The application of these stages, how they unfold, and their impact on each individual show that we all grieve differently and in our own way. Grieving is a personal thing and there's no wrong or right way to deal with grief. Grief is the hard work of accepting the loss you've experienced.

You may jump from one stage to another and then back again, skip a stage, or even combine stages. The intensity of these emotions during and after your loved one passes can also include numbness and disbelief. You've just witnessed death and experienced the shock of that final separating moment from someone who was very close to you. For some, the grieving process may take a few months; for others, it may take a few years. While it may be tempting to push past these intense emotional responses, remember: don't rush grief in trying to get over it.

There'll also probably be some depression that accompanies grieving. These feelings could be mild or intense and range all the way from hopelessness, fatigue, and sadness to loss of appetite, loss of interest in going out, and loss of optimism in general. Hopefully these bouts of depression will pass quickly and not become acute. A little bit of depression is natural because you identified yourself in some way with the person who has passed—your spouse, your child, your mother, your father, your grandmother, your grandfather, your sister, your brother, or . . . (you fill in the blank). Their passing leaves an undeniable void in your life.

If these feelings of depression persist or become severe, please seek professional help to sort out your feelings. It's important to receive guidance for coping with grief in a healthy and helpful way. There are also many support group options, such as the biblically based *GriefShare* program, that are focused on navigating the grieving process.

As you learn to deal with this empty feeling, you will need to redefine who you are without the person you cared for so deeply. You've lost your familiar grounding and may find yourself at loose ends. Pray for guidance as God helps you decide how to fill this void in your life. In the midst of these uncertainties, remember the comforting words found in John 14:27: "Do not let your hearts be troubled and do not be afraid." During this time of searching, remember that God is your help. He is the one who sustains you (Psalm 54:4).

Doubts may remain as you ask yourself, "Could I or should I have done anything differently?" Just as in your caregiving journey, your vitals and dependables will probably be by your side, helping you deal with these questions. Then, when you least expect it, your constants will just seem to miraculously appear, offering comfort and reassurance. Be willing to freely share your feelings with everyone who was intimately involved in your journey.

Even when you think you're in control again, there'll be dates on the calendar, songs, sounds, sights, smells, settings, pictures, and people that trigger emotional memories of your loved one. Something as simple as notes on cards and messages of condolences from well-wishers can bring comfort or reignite the pain of loss. Tears can begin to flow again as you soak in these heartfelt words. Sometimes you'll know when a trigger is coming, but it can also happen when least expected.

The first time you do something that you'd always done together is sure to be a trigger. Things that should've been easy for me to do unexpectedly caught me by surprise. The first time

I walked through the front door of the church and sat down alone brought back a flood of memories and tears that continued throughout the service. The same was also true when stepping into our favorite restaurant and being seated at a table for one for the first time. Being a solo visitor to friends and relatives, especially to Gwen's younger sister, always brought back vivid memories and many more uncontrollable tears.

No matter how near or distant these triggered memories are from your time of loss, they can still bring teary eyes or a lump to your throat that is hard to swallow. Don't fight these feelings. Tears are a natural part of the grieving and healing process, helping to wash away the pain of loss. Remember, tears can be refreshing and shouldn't be avoided.

Sharing Your Story

What you've learned and experienced as a caregiver can be an invaluable resource to others. We found that any time we got two or more caregivers together (no matter what type of caregiving situation they were dealing with), it wasn't long before they began sharing and discovering common experiences. It was heartwarming to listen to their stories of struggles, triumphs, and joys. Many of their stories had common themes. They were eager to share helpful caregiving hints and inspirational examples of how their faith allowed them to persevere no matter what obstacles they encountered. They were keenly aware of God's presence in their lives and in the lives of those they cared for. It became apparent that sharing their experiences gave them joy!

You have the same opportunity to share these similar types of positive memories. You may not be ready now, but there will be a time when you'll be able to easily share these experiences and memories. When this time comes, it will feel good knowing that your experiences can comfort and help others. By sharing the hope and assurance you found in God's blessings during your journey, you can be an inspiration and a source of knowledge for others who face similar challenges.

If you don't think you're ready or able to open yourself up to discussing your experiences with others, then you may want to take time to capture some of your thoughts through journaling. There's no wrong or right way to journal and no prescribed method of journaling. Use it as a personal sounding board to capture and express your innermost thoughts through writing while they are fresh in your mind.

One caregiver described how she kept a journal throughout her caregiving journey where she jotted down notes about her time with God and all she was experiencing. She would date each entry, pour out her thoughts, and then end by writing out her prayer requests. As she saw the answers to these prayers, she would add them to her journal. This helped her process her hopes, anger, fears, frustrations, longings, gratitude, and joys. It gave her peace of mind as she became aware of God's presence and guidance. By rereading and reflecting on her journal entries after her mother's death, she was strengthened and comforted. These written reminders helped her to easily share with others her stories of God's faithfulness throughout her journey.

Reflecting on all of your experiences and being willing to share what you've learned helps in processing your thoughts and emotions. Your vitals or constants will probably always be there with reminders and stories, helping to keep your loved one's memory alive. Others may be hesitant to bring up discussions about their memories of your loved one. You can help open the door for them to share their memories by talking openly about your own memories, especially pleasant ones. In addition, these sharing times give them opportunities to also process their grief.

You've turned the page to a new chapter in your life, so start making new memories. It's okay to weave in fond memories and stories of your loved one into conversations. People enjoy hearing these stories about things that mean so much to you.

However, be careful not to overdo it. Look for a balance in your life between the past and the future. As you develop new friendships or strengthen old ones, you can begin exploring and settling into new routines.

Move on with Hope

Don't lose sight of the fact that you've been on a sacred journey. You faithfully persevered on this caregiving journey. You poured yourself into this role. It will always be an important part of your life. Judges 5:21 says, "March on, my soul; be strong." Hold these words close to your heart. God has been with you every step of the way. He will continue to be with you as you face the future. He is your shepherd and will care for you. He goes before you, giving you guidance, strength, hope, and comfort. He is still intimately involved in every detail of your life.

It is through faith that you can hold onto God's promises. You'll find the peace as well as the strength, courage, and boldness to face each day. It is your hope and faith that reassures you of seeing your loved one again in heaven. Hebrews 11:1 says, "Faith is being sure of what we hope for and certain of what we do not see." You need not be afraid; God is present to comfort you now and in the days ahead.

Catherine's niece, Elizabeth, who lost her battle with leukemia, relied on many favorite Bible verses throughout her struggles. One particular verse had a very special meaning to her. It was Hebrews 10:23. She was especially fond of a paraphrased version of that verse that goes something like this:

Don't let go of the hope your faith has given you.
Cherish it.
Seize it and hold it tight.
Put your hope in what God has promised you;
for He is reliable, trustworthy, and faithful to His Word.

Soon after Elizabeth passed away, this verse became a favorite of Catherine's sister as she learned to move on with hope in God. She found this verse written in calligraphy and hung it on her kitchen wall. It serves as a constant reminder of God's promises to always be with her. It helps her remember His presence and that He is leading her and guiding her. She knows that God, who was faithful in the past, will be faithful in the future.

God promises to always be with you, too. As you move forward, He will enable you, guide you, and continue to direct you in your journey as you heal from your loss. The Irish folk worship band Rend Collective reminds us with their lyrics in "My Lighthouse" that God is our lighthouse. He promises to carry you safe to shore. You don't need to fear what tomorrow brings. As you look to Him, He will lead you and give you peace.

As you look to God as your lighthouse, may you be a reflection of His blessings in your life. Your words and actions can be a bright, shining light, offering reassuring guidance, help, and comfort to others in their time of need. When you have hope, it wells up inside you and overflows to others. Romans 15:13 says, "May the God of hope fill you with all joy and peace as you trust in him, so that you may overflow with hope by the power of the Holy Spirit." You can share this hope and peace with others.

Thank you for joining us on our journey as we described the process of what it means to embrace a faith-based approach to intentional caregiving. Thank you for slipping your hand into God's as you partnered with Him in caring for your loved one. May it be said of you, "It is obvious you truly cared for your loved one."

* * * * *

Pause for Prayer

Dear Lord, as I move forward without my loved one, thank You that You are with me as my reassuring anchor during these difficult and uncertain times. Help me to remember that You are with me and that I don't need to fear what tomorrow brings. Help me to find joy and fulfillment as I keep my eyes on You. Help me to know how You want me to live the rest of my life. Give me the strength and courage to face the challenges of each day. Amen.

The Lord bless you and keep you;
The Lord make his face to shine upon you,
and be gracious to you;
The Lord lift up his countenance upon you,
and give you peace.
(Numbers 6:24–26 NRSV)

Appendixes

Appendix A

Legal and Estate Documents

Place a check mark beside the document once it has been completed.

- ☐ **Last Will and Testament**: This legal document designates who receives assets held solely in your name at time of death. It also appoints an individual or individuals to oversee the distribution of those assets.
- ☐ **Living Will (Advance Directive)**: This legal document communicates to doctors and other healthcare professionals the kind of healthcare you desire when you are no longer able to communicate your desires.
- ☐ **Durable Power of Attorney**: This legal document allows an individual to handle your finances. Only someone you completely trust should be named in this document.
- ☐ **Health Care Surrogate:** This legal document allows an individual to make health, medical, and surgical decisions

for you if you become incompetent or disabled and cannot make decisions for yourself.

☐ **HIPAA Form**: This legal document allows designated people to have access to your medical information and records. It is not a decision making document, but instead a document that allows the release of health information.

☐ **Declaration Naming Preneed Guardian**: This legal document allows you to designate an individual to act as your guardian in the event anyone ever initiates incompetency and guardianship proceedings against you.

Depending on your circumstances, you may also want to consider having one or all of the following documents.

☐ **Revocable Trust**: This legal document manages and protects assets, providing flexibility and income to the living grantor; he or she is able to adjust the provisions of the trust and earned income, knowing that the estate will be transferred upon death.

☐ **Organ Donor Registration**: If you want to be an organ donor, you can make your wishes known and documented by joining an organ donor registry. The easiest way to do this is to have it noted on your driver's license or state issued identification card. You should also let your wishes be known to family members and your primary healthcare provider.

☐ **Medicare Authorization to Disclose Personal Information Form**: This document only applies to individuals receiving Medicare benefits. It allows designated individuals to have access to personal health information related to Medicare.

Appendix B

Financial Accounts

Place a check mark beside each of the following accounts and make sure the appropriate name(s) is on each one.

☐ Brokerage and Trading Accounts
☐ Checking and Savings Accounts
☐ Credit Card Accounts
☐ Debit Card Accounts
☐ 401k Accounts
☐ IRA Accounts
☐ Pension Accounts
☐ Safe Deposit Box Account and Keys

Appendix C

Other Important Documents

Place a check mark beside each document once it is up to date and has been placed in an accessible location.

☐ Automobile Insurances Policies
☐ Birth Certificate(s)
☐ Homeowners (Flood and Windstorm) Insurance Policies
☐ House/Land/Cemetery Deeds
☐ Long-term Care Policies
☐ Marriage License and/or Divorce Decree
☐ Medical and Life Insurance Policies
☐ Prepaid Funeral Policies
☐ Vehicle Titles and Registrations

Appendix D

Funeral Planning Questions

- What funeral home will be used?
- Will an obituary be written ahead of time?
- Where will the obituary be published?
- Where will the service(s) be held?
- Who will conduct the service(s)?
- What Scripture verses will be read?
- What songs will be sung?
- Will there be special musical performances?
- Who else will speak and share memories?
- Will there be a reception after the service?
- Will there be a graveside service?
- Will there be an open or closed casket?
- Will there be an option for sending flowers?
- Where would your loved one like donations to be sent in their memory?
- Do honor arrangements need to be made for recognitions such as military, masons, eastern star, elks, etc.?
- Will there be an additional gathering after the formal reception for family, relatives, and close friends?

Notes

1. Adele Ahlberg Calhoun, *Spiritual Disciplines Handbook: Practices that Transform Us, Revised and Expanded (Downers Grove, IL: IVP Books, 2015).*

2. *Richard Foster, Celebration of Discipline: The Path to Spiritual Growth (San Francisco: Harper, 1998).*

3. *Reinhold Niebuhr, The Essential Reinhold Niebuhr: Selected Essays and Addresses: New Edition* (Yale University Press, 1987).

4. Kara Tippets and Jill Lynn Buteyn, *Just Show Up: The Dance of Walking Through Suffering Together (Colorado Springs, CO: David C. Cook, 2015).*

5. *Elisabeth Kubler-Ross, On Death and Dying (New York: The Macmillan Company, 1969).*

6. *Catherine Marshall, Beyond Our Selves (New York: McGraw-Hill Book Company, Inc., 1961).*

About the Authors

After successful careers in the hospitality industry and higher education, Dr. Roy Cook devoted his attention to caring for his wife, Gwen, who struggled with Parkinson's disease for fifteen years. Through their love for each other and their trust in God, they found the inspiration and hope to face each new challenge. After listening to numerous stories of how others navigated their caregiving challenges, Roy felt called to share these collective insights with a broader audience. Since he has published several successful books and numerous academic papers, it seemed only natural to do this by writing *Reassuring Guidance: A Faith-Based Caregiving Resource*.

Catherine Hilliard is a pastor's wife who has served in ministry with her husband, Ron Hilliard, for forty-five years at First Presbyterian Church in North Palm Beach, Florida. She is a trained Stephen's Minister, having firsthand experience of walking along with others in their times of suffering and need. She has taught numerous spiritual formation classes, incorporating the spiritual practices of prayer, silence, solitude, rest, peace, knowing God's presence, and worship. As she took care of her mother for over ten years, she experienced the important role faith has in being equipped to be the best caregiver you can be.

Printed in the United States
by Baker & Taylor Publisher Services